Irene van Lippe-Bieste...
— a short biography

1. Chronology

The Netherlands, 1938. Princess Juliana, the only daughter of Queen Wilhelmina and Crown Princess, gives birth to her firstborn, Princess Beatrix.

Europe, 1939. Nazi Germany invades Poland and everyone in the United Kingdom, France and neighbouring countries now fears that an all-out war is unavoidable. Princess Juliana and Prince Bernard van Lippe-Biesterfeld's second child is born, and they decide to name her Irene, after the Greek goddess of peace.

1940. The Nazis invade the Netherlands, as well as Belgium and half of France, and Princess Juliana flees to Ottawa, Canada. Naturally, Irene goes too — her bullet-proof cradle is now in a museum in Apeldoorn. But during the next few years her father is in Europe fighting, and she misses him intensely.

1945. The royal family returns home — but it is not home for the little princess whose birthday garden-party is attended by 6,000 children.

1963–64. Irene provokes a constitutional crisis, first by converting to Catholicism, and then by marrying Carlist claimant to the Spanish throne Prince Carlos Hugo de Bourbon–Parma. The whole affair makes the headlines in the Dutch press over several months as it involves multiple crisis cabinet meetings, the opposition of the Dutch parliament and a papal audience. It culminates in a marriage ceremony in Rome attended by ex-Empress Zita of Austria–Hungary and various members of the Spanish, French and Italian nobility — but not one member of the Dutch royal family or any Dutch diplomatic representative. Thus Irene renounces her right of succession to the throne of Orange and chooses not to live in the Netherlands.

Irene moves to General Franco's Spain and gets involved in the free-dom movement fighting for democracy. She also works actively with underprivileged women in Madrid's poorer quarters.

Carlos and Irene have four children: Carlos (1970), Jaime (1972), Margarita (1972) and Carolina (1974).

1981. Irene divorces Carlos and returns to live in the Netherlands, a single mother with four children to raise.

October 1995. *Dialogue With Nature* is published in the Netherlands with a launch party in Utrecht attended by Irene's mother, the ex-Queen Juliana, and Irene's younger sister, Princess Margriet, as well as her own four children. In all, there are some sixty people present and they all take part in the short meditation led by Irene who invites them to visualise a tree and ask it what it has to say to them.

2. Spiritual biography

Quite early on, Irene learns to escape her golden cage by taking refuge in nature and communing with the trees and plants. Surrounded by stern adults who ignore her violent migraines, she feels very lonely and quite miserable, although she always appears in public with a radiant smile. There is such a gap between the image of 'the glamorous Princess of the Netherlands', as the Dutch press nickname her, and the reality of a woman who feels abandoned at every step of her life, and in particular at the time of her marriage and then of her divorce.

One day, she decides to make a completely new beginning and starts working on herself, taking various personal development workshops in the US and Europe and partaking of all kinds of therapy and complementary treatment. And her connection with nature deepens further as she exchanges messages with trees and plants, with animals — in particular dolphins — and even with the sun.

Her friends do not really understand but in Irene's experience most people living in urban conditions have lost their connection with nature and it is her hope that this book will be of help, whatever the reason for which it was originally purchased. Her advice is to allow peace and quiet in our busy lives and thus realise that we are part of a much larger whole than the limited perception of our five senses would seem to indicate.

In *Dialogue With Nature*, Irene fearlessly shares her most intimate feelings. Her courage is truly remarkable.

Dialogue With Nature

Dialogue With Nature

Irene van Lippe-Biesterfeld
Princess Irene of the Netherlands

Translated from the Dutch by Beatrix Descamps

FINDHORN
Press

Published by
Findhorn Press
The Park, Findhorn
Forres IV36 0TZ
Scotland
tel +44 (0)1309 690582/fax 690036
e-mail: thierry@findhorn.org
http://www.gaia.org/findhornpress/

Contents

Dedicated to nature's creatures, to the dolphins, to my children and other dear ones. And to an old friend who cherishes the dream of a world in which Mankind will be known as Kindman on the planet of Kindness.

Foreword

Whoever writes an autobiographical book, whatever its message, lives in a dangerous world. From the day of publication, she has to deal with people who know more about her than she does about them. In one step she emerges from the protective armour which a lifetime of experience and intuition has built up around her ego. It requires courage and confidence, and powerful motivation. Princess Irene has taken this step, and all that I have written above refers to her.

From the beginning I have been against it. After reading the manuscript my resistance is undiminished. Not because Irene van Lippe-Biesterfeld indulges in frivolous revelations; on the contrary, *Dialogue With Nature*, in stylish and often poetic language, describes her search for the essence of the cosmos and everything that lives and grows, leading to a philosophical approach that sees contact with nature as the source, an uplifting, sometimes baffling but always interesting revelation. Even so, it is an extremely personal experience which exposes the soul, however indirectly, like unlocking a door after which it is not always easy to keep potential intruders from entering the premises. Publishing a book inevitably leads to the media, the realm of the best-trained intruders in the business, for whom the entire edifice of Irene's life, past, present and future, is fair game. As a lifelong journalist, proud of his profession, I only hope that they will welcome her warmly as a colleague.

Clearly, she has not paid the slightest attention to my negative advice. This is not surprising, as she knows what she wants and fears no one. Only a bold spirit would ask an outspoken critic to write a foreword to her book. However, as a woman of the world, she knows quite well that a positive word from an opponent far outweighs the praises of a supporter, and friendly contact with metaphysics is not part of my reputation. But am I really such an outsider in Irene's territory? After all, I was born in Java, where humanity lacks the Western arrogance of according an immortal soul only to itself. And didn't the dolphins of Kealakekua Bay, Hawaii, accept both of us as their playmates?

I understand the reason for her determination very well and do not lack admiration for it: Irene is in the process of developing a vision of life which, personally as well as cosmically, promises hope for the future. But in order to have an effect, something which to her is already crystal clear must be understood and practised by many others. She can contribute to this by sharing her experiences. The facts presented in this book are of less importance in this respect as they often consist of personal interpretations of emotional observations, but cumulatively they point the way to a shining vision for those who are willing and able to approach these controversial concepts with an open mind. Considering the condition of the world and the behaviour of humanity, I can only applaud this.

In fact, I am the prototype of the reader at whom *Dialogue With Nature* is aimed: one person out of many concerned about the fate of the world and all its living elements, who see the problems but not the solutions, for which they hopefully await someone else's inspiration. It is this kind of inspiration that has motivated Irene to write her book, as her love for nature and everything 'soul-full' — for her an unlimited concept — is genuine and deep. This love the book projects, not in order to convert the reader but to share Irene's experience honestly and without prejudice. It is a generous gift, limited only by the receptivity of those who may benefit from it.

Be prepared for surprises. Time and again ostensible details lead to unexpected insights, familiar situations to distant views of unknown territory, observations to concepts on the verge of fantasy, for everyone according to their attitude and imagination. The final result is a vision of two realities, the worldly and the metaphysical, which the author has managed to balance successfully, in her own life as well. *Dialogue With Nature* is a bold step towards a worthy goal and in it Irene guides you by the hand through this stirring phase of her extraordinary life.

Captain Erik Hazelhoff, RMWO, DFC
Former ADC to HM Queen Wilhelmina

Prelude

Many people deny the existence
of everything they cannot perceive.
Speak only their own language.
Have no respect for what they don't understand.

'Common sense'
once understood the world
was flat,
you couldn't leave the earth.
you couldn't split atoms.
Everything seemed different.
Everything will always seem different.
Realities never imagined
become facts,
which in their turn become senseless:
Everything moves in everything,
is cause
of everything.
Luckily there are more and more people amongst us
who have the courage
not to keep quiet any more
about what for many is a threat.
Like death
before life,
the most natural thing in the world.
For how can you cut down a tree
when you know it has a soul?
How can you kill a dolphin
when you know he can talk?

What does measuring mean
when you can travel through time
in the blink of an eye?
Are you awake
when you deny
that dreams are much needed?

In this book Irene van Lippe-Biesterfeld
writes freely
about her experiences
in this bewildering world
where there are no limits to the possible.
She teaches us
that the only limit you have to overcome
is the one within yourself.

Herman van Veen

PART ONE

1. Memories

Do not dally collecting flowers to preserve them, but keep going, for all along your path flowers will grow.

Rabindranath Tagore, *Wandering Birds*

Ειρηνη, peace, I was named, in the hope that war would not break out. At six months old and to the sound of bombing, I was put on the boat in a bullet-proof cradle, the cradle I know only from the museum of the 'Palace het Loo' in Apeldoorn. The ship, the *Sumatra*, I also know only from stories. With my mother and my eldest little sister we sailed that whole ocean to Canada because there was a war and *we* had to be spared. I was my mother's second daughter. My father's name I chose to bear only much later. My mother was the only child of Wilhelmina, Queen of the Netherlands. Far away from the reality of Holland I had my first experiences of life in a country of undulating green and space and quiet. We lived in a residential area of Ottawa in a villa with two columns by the front door and a garden with a swing. I slept upstairs in a small bed with bars you could climb on. Only the radio in the big sitting room told us about the horrors back home in the Netherlands. The faces of the grown-ups, who never seemed to be able to sit down while they listened to it because of the enormous tension that built up around that small set, told me, the little girl, that something terrible and incredibly big was going on, somewhere out there where we actually belonged. My father was a German Dutchman who dropped bombs on Germany from an aeroplane. He did this from London where he had taken refuge as my grandmother had done. The 'grown-ups' were afraid he would perish — that also came out of that radio. I missed him terribly. He came to see us a few times and I didn't understand why he left me again. Nobody told me that even when you are far away you can still love somebody.

I guess it was around 1944, I must have been about five years old. One luminous white blossom surrounded by green leaves against a hard blue sky. The image had such an impact on me that today it is still etched on my retina and in my soul. It was the tree on a corner of the street I walked along daily on my way to nursery school, an extra pair of small knickers in a little bag because I always wet my pants. Images coloured red by the 'Indian summer'. Playing naked in the grass where we jumped through the water of the sprinkler on steaming hot days. Santa Claus who scared me stiff. Playing blind man's buff, hitting my head against one of those columns daubed with nasty small stones, suddenly covered with blood and ruining the best suit of Mr Knauer, the detective, for he carried me upstairs to bed.

1945. Back to the Netherlands on the luxury liner the *Queen Elizabeth*, I was scared. They had told me all kind of stories about the country we were returning to. A couple of times, in deadly fear, I had hidden myself in the coalshed in order to escape the obligatory injections we seemed to need in order to live in that country we were going to. There were terrible diseases there and everything was very bad. Via England, where we played hide and seek for a while in big haystacks, we arrived by aeroplane. A broadly smiling gentleman, who worked with my grandmother because he had become a hero in the war, helped us out of the aeroplane.

To reach the house we were now going to live in, we had to go through an impressive gate before which stood a friendly man in uniform. It was a much, much bigger house than the one in Ottawa and it stretched out like a white fan among the greenery. Between that gate with the man in uniform and the house stretched grass lawns with neat paths cut through them. A few stately hundred-year-old beeches made the view even more enticing. Behind the house we found a beautiful big garden with giant rhododendron bushes full of rabbits, a gigantic pond with a fountain metres high, a rowing boat and woods to wander in and get lost. We hid, explored and climbed trees.

On my sixth birthday, there are six thousand children in the garden. Where was I myself? Who did this garden belong to and what did it mean to be a little princess? Where did all those children live?

I now slept in a big room with a high ceiling and high windows. We had a super bath. You had to climb three steps to get into it and you could play in it with all your little sisters and friends, it was that big and deep! We ran through the long corridors and up and down the big staircases, excited at having so much space.

Circa 1952. A hiding place there in the woods of Soestdijk, for that was the name of the palace. Feeling the wood of the plank bridge under my knees, the water coloured brown by fallen, quietly rotting leaves that lay there on the bottom below. Over the wide ditch that ends up in the big pond, an elegant white bridge. Reflections of birches and beeches, sounds of birds and leaves in the wind, sun on the water, insects, daddy-long-legs that draw little ripples like their own small worlds. My own place to dream away in and to be myself. Alone. There I receive comfort and rest and I am safe. I suck up smells, colours and sounds through my senses and give these encounters and images a place deep inside me, so that my heart, my belly, my eyes and ears are filled with them.

1953. Laying the foundation stone of the Dutch church, the Austin Friars, in London. A small girl still who is carrying out her first official function. Small gloves and a little hat, grey coat over a wide skirt. Little white socks in little black shoes with a small strap. I have to step forward, outside the circle of people I don't know, and end up all alone in an open space, amidst all those friendly but curious strangers. Too young still and too unprepared for such intrusive curiosity, for the expectations of all these people who pretend to know who this little princess is — who I am. Scared stiff to get it wrong. Panic! And yet again there is nobody to tell me what I need to know. Eyes, yes, lots of them, and opinions about that little girl. In the middle of the open space there is a tree. I feel that this tree is the only one who sees who I am. I hear him say: 'Come and sit under me, you can play, there are little friends for you here who also like to play.' But the grown-ups don't hear this and are thinking of other things like the building of that church. And they don't know that the comfort this church is supposed to offer people is already to be found near the tree.

From that moment on there has always been a tree with which I have been safe. Under which I could for ever be a child, be myself, play. Since then I have had a true communion with trees. I have known their protection, their acceptance of how I am, in contrast to how I should be.

Taloutje, who also was in London during the war as one of my grandmother's ladies-in-waiting, sits by my bed and reads to me. For me she is like that sweet fairy from the Walt Disney film *Cinderella* who can cast spells on everything with her magic wand. Grimm's fairy tales come to life through her. *Is* she the fairy and *am* I the little princess . . . ? How do you get out of a fairy tale? Who makes up the fairy tale? Who sets the rules?

I also remember the long holidays in the mountains. Swirling snow, my skis point themselves straight down, into the abyss. My weight a little to the right, then to the left again, I bounce as if in slow motion through fresh powder snow, one metre thick; it flies over me and fills my mouth and ears. It's so much like a feeling of flying. All body, through the playful exertion of the sport and the freedom of movement and air and sun and white and blue. Straight ahead, straight down!

A dog is barking out there, somewhere beyond the gates. Every night I hear him. Who lives there and what does their house look like? I would so much like to know how the people in those streets and houses live. What are they like and what do they do? I would love to play with the children. I hate the fence that stands between the 'others' and me.

2. Towards a New Balance

You believe Divine Oneness sees and judges people. We think
of Divine Oneness as feeling the intent and emotion of beings.
Not as interested in what we do as why we do it.

Ooota, from *Mutant Messages from Down Under*

Madrid. It is a very dry time in my life, on the bare plateau of
Castilia there are no trees except the chestnut tree in my bed-
room painted by my grandmother. The image of the proud
white candles amidst the green leaves conveys at least the idea
of humidity in the extreme climate of this dried-out land. I am
married to a foreigner full of ideals. I am like that too and together we think we can make the world a little bit better. Inde-
structible youth! Every now and then Carlos and I go to an
oasis where we can fill our lungs with green. A respite in a time
of indefatigable giving and giving up for an ideal. Into a piece
of world weighed down by fascism we hoped to be able to
bring a system in which people could express and make their
own decisions. Believing in human worth was the name of
that ideal. But how can people experience their own worth
when they have been considered worthless for so long within a suppressive political system? The time wasn't yet ripe for
such a big shift. Our work failed because of this. And so did
our marriage, but for other reasons.

It was time to separate. We had done our absolute best.
Together we had four wonderful children. But when you

make working for an ideal a priority so that it absorbs you completely, demands everything of you, then it can happen that your marriage dries up as a result. Precisely because you have given everything, that separation is tough and bitter. It tears you apart in every way.

I think a divorce is always terrible. The disappointment that it didn't work is enormous. Your children's secure world gets shattered. Their confusion is total. Pain — deep, consuming, despairing pain. The sorrow and the lack of understanding around you about your decision to go on alone make everything even worse. And I had no idea whether I could manage on my own. It was a hard time during which I made new choices. Thus I decided to use my father's name from then on, like everybody else in the Netherlands. I plunged into Further Education, something I had wanted to do for a long time — I chose Women and Well-Being. It is an adult education course providing the opportunity to support adults going through processes of change. I had experienced at first hand the problems women from different cultures encounter in this Western society and I had written a book about it. That's why I continued to focus further on that group. In Madrid I had started women's groups in the suburbs where migrants from various parts of the country lived in difficult circumstances. Loneliness, poverty, disorientation, ignorance. In the Netherlands, in between my political work, I had done a course for trainers to assist groups, at that time called 'Women Orient Themselves to Society'. This had seemed to me a first step towards helping women acquire a self-image with which they might more easily get a grip on their own lives. I and a group of female social workers, whom I in my turn had trained in the methods, took to the districts, usually followed by the Spanish secret police, who thought we were communists because we worked with women in the poorest quarters. It was difficult but invigorating work and we had fun. I'll never forget the hour-long discussions we had with women from all political parties in small, smoke-filled back rooms (for in those days all meetings were still illegal). It was as if we were discovering the world anew. What did we ourselves want as women? What was our own opinion about things?

I am allergic to injustice. We had already fought against that in Spain. Now, in my 'new' independent life, this striving assumed a whole new significance. Whereas before I had committed myself via my husband, I now wanted to become better acquainted with myself and my self-worth in order to understand and assist others more effectively. I wanted to be closer to myself and to my fellow human beings. No more barriers because of my origin, my political role as 'wife of', and all that kind of inhibiting separation. Nor did I want any more of the political-structural approach. I don't know whether the world can change but I am convinced that people can. I yearned for a person-to-person approach. How often I had observed in fascination the changes that can take place in a person. What I equally learned to understand is that when people live in a more conscious and balanced way because they don't hide their inner wounds and pain but look them in the eye and process them, they not only have a tremendous influence on their surroundings but on the cosmic whole as well. I see the human 'species' as one large body, with every single person a cell of that body. If one cell feels good in itself, and is healthy and contented with itself and its life, then this is vitally important for the whole body. And the healthier this 'whole body' is, the more beneficial it is for our environment, for nature.

There I was, back in the Netherlands after seventeen years, in a circle of women from all strata of society. It was like jumping into the deep end, in a country I had never really learned to know. 'Trix is nix'* said a badge on the dungarees of one of the women . . . I broke out in a cold sweat at the aggression I felt behind this. Will *I* be accepted here? During the first round of getting to know each other I asked the group to give me a chance to be myself and not to see me as a representative of the royal house as an institution. The circle closed around me, I was given the chance.

---

* Trix = abbreviation of Beatrix, Queen of the Netherlands. Therefore 'Beatrix is nothing'.

The training involved a lot of self-analysis, in fact you could not avoid yourself, and we did a lot of crying! By this means we cleansed ourselves on the inside. Class barriers got broken down, the preconceptions, pain and anger about them were worked through, and analyses of society and one's own purposes became clearer. To combine motherhood and work was quite a task for all the women with children. Too little time, divided attention and loyalties, a crazy amount of responsibility. At one time we had to reserve one shift per week just for ourselves . . . We had a fit of giggles. Every quarter of an hour of my day was planned.

During that time I did everything alone: taking the children to school, shopping, learning to do the housework (I had never learned to use a vacuum cleaner, for instance, and didn't know you had to put a bag in the thing to get a result!), training, working, grieving.

Learning to find my way in my own country. It is unthinkable now but in this country I had never driven a car alone. Always there had been either a driver or a detective with me and he would know the way or was supposed to know it at least. When after the training sessions I walked back to my car across the canals of Amsterdam, I felt I consisted of several parts. The working woman in a real world who nevertheless became unreal because she was the princess who was brought up outside of things and thus didn't really belong to that world. By the end of the training I had grown into one whole being. What became equally clear to me during that time was that women can turn out to be the best and most flexible of managers, because they have to operate on so many fronts at once.

This training also had a political aspect but the emphasis lay more on the human being in her or his social context, while in the political work we had busied ourselves with humankind in terms of ideas. Now we did not lose sight of what is inevitable, in other words the structural perspective of how class barriers function and what place in society is meted out to you if you are a woman.

In those days I lived in a white house at a busy crossroads

in Soest. I remember how at night I went to look at the children one by one. How proud I was of them and how incredibly happy that they were with me, in my house. I was so much stronger on my own than I had ever suspected I could be.

Another part of the training was practical. In Utrecht I assisted Spanish women in their process of conscious awakening; they had enormous problems with the balance between their own culture and life in the Netherlands, where they had been living for seventeen years, as long as I had been married! Later on I started developing this work and together with Lydia I founded ISIS, an institute for training, advice and coaching for managers and teams. We chose that name after some hesitation as we thought it might be too 'soft' for a business. But because the goddess Isis stands for life and I myself feel extremely drawn to her life dynamics — the positive energy that can bring life to seemingly dead-end situations — we used it anyway. It was a strong starting point, if nothing else! Now it is called ISIS, Institute for Transcultural Development.

At ISIS the basic idea is that we can learn from each other through our differences. In particular the arrival of people with a wholly different culture, with their own specific living and working habits, can cause you to reflect on your own habits and how much space you have for each other's 'being different'. Therefore it is useful to understand to what extent your education determines your behaviour and how your culture and subculture (for instance class background, church) play an influential role in this. It gives new insights and offers new perspectives. Ultimately, a lot of cultures together are more fascinating than one alone! That is the principle of synergy. Together we are more than the sum of the parts would lead us to believe. The norms and values of one culture can be new and instructive for another. Thus all cultures have something unique to offer each other, and within them every human being is unique in turn, for naturally in our own culture or subculture each of us is totally different from other people. It is stretching and stimulating to live and work with others who think differently from what you are used to, and to examine what you take for granted. Later on these insights and experiences helped me to go a step further. I understood that diversity of life in its widest sense, or 'nature', has as much to teach us as do cultures and that the synergy of the interplay of all that lives on this earth makes a beautiful whole in which everything counts.

For me it is extremely important that everyone has the right not only to claim their own place and sound their own note but equally to learn how to do it. All voices are necessary, precisely because we are all different. The voices of the Ancient Peoples, whether they be the North American Indians, the Pygmies or the Mayans, the Aboriginals or the Inuit (Eskimos), have something to say, nowadays more than ever, now that the balance is so thoroughly disturbed. As such they can tell us about how to deal with nature as an equal. By this I don't mean to imply that we have to go back to the past. We are after all not Indians or Mayans or Aboriginals. From my point of view there is no sense whatsoever in imitating them nostalgically because that would not fit in with our reality. You are yourself and never somebody else. We can learn from the old wisdom and integrate it into our present reality to find a new balance with all the knowledge of our technological consciousness.

During our time in Spain we had already abandoned the fatalistic idea that 'God determines whether someone is rich or poor'. Those were dangerous images instilled in us to keep us in our place. But we still hang onto them. As Westerners, for instance, we still assume that we are superior, that we know more and better, that we should and can make decisions for others. Even though you think you don't play this game, you are still imbued with that attitude of superiority as a result of your schooling, history books, the media and the general thought-forms. Unconsciously, yes. When you do become conscious of it, it is a big step in the direction of equality. According to some, the mere fact of having more money would give our Western cultures certain rights. To give assistance from 'on high' is condescending and can be terribly insulting. It denies the other their human dignity. 'Social pornography' it was called recently by a Guatemalan liberty fighter, who said that paternalistic 'help' did more harm than the hunger people experienced. When your dignity as a human being is not recognised or, worse still, is taken from you, there is little left. To regard those with less money and opportunities as poor devils, that really is degrading! To cooperate, to complement each other, is something else. To give precisely that which the other indicates they need is excellent. To regard the other as less is terrible. It is all about respect and learning from each other. Being open to each other's wisdom and uniqueness, whether between human beings and nature or between cultures. In nature everything knows its own value. People have lost that understanding. That is why, in our Western culture, it is no small task to learn to experience your own worth once more and to live from that. Over and over again I have experienced this in my political work and in working with groups of people in the process of change.

This worth as a human being, what happens to it when you are dead? What comes after all this? And is there anything before it? That there is something before and after this life, I know for sure, don't ask me how. Intuition? Do I know something through former experiences? Former lives? In my work I always see the enormous arsenal of positive power that exists in people. For me it is a feast to witness an individual contacting that power. Where does that life-force go when you are no longer here? To heaven as the churches say? And then what happens there? Do we all sit there together, beaming at each other and twiddling our thumbs? . . . No, we won't have those any more. What do we do then? Do we haunt the living because we love them or want to pester them? Is there a God

or something like it? How shall I imagine it? Is there a hierarchy? I don't like that idea.

All through my adult education training and in all my work
there was always in the background the certainty that what we
are doing here has repercussions on the greater whole. That
therefore it is important to work through painful situations
rather than around them. As a young girl I knew for certain
that there was something like a greater interrelationship.
Already at that time I experienced it as a central source of
power, of life, like a warm friendship really that I had with . . .
well, with what I didn't know. With something sweet somewhere out there among the stars.

I embarked on a search for that essence, that source. My
desire to be closer to it was on my mind throughout everything. With all the questions that come with it. What is there
behind all visible things? What is it all about? Why so much
injustice, why so much division between people? What is the
meaning of life, of my life? I could gaze at the stars for hours
and passionately wish to be in contact with that warm 'something' out there in that immense void. I read about it, discussed
it, searched for it, wished myself part of it.

In the guest room Elsie opened her trunk and, under my aston-
ished eyes, took out a small table. She put it up somewhat
impatiently and placed a chair on each side of it. 'I want to let
you get to know your guide, sit down.' As if relishing the effect
a carefully chosen present can have, she motioned me to a
chair. I had read articles she had published about her experiences with her guides. She described them as beings who

accompany each person as helpers and protectors. Souls who are not incarnated in a body and who stay around you with their energy. So, ghosts after all. Reading about her contacts with guides I found the idea of such beings an engaging possibility, maybe even a possible reality.

Now here in my own house she was going to bring me into contact with my guides! I had not been able to prepare myself for this at all, insofar as one can prepare for such a thing. What lay in wait for me? Would I see or hear anything? I felt my own excitement and tension and was extremely curious about how she was going to handle the process.

She sat down too, on the chair opposite me, and asked aloud for the name of my guide. To my utmost surprise the table started to move, and she counted up to twenty-six. She wrote down the letter 'z' and explained that every movement of the table was one letter of the alphabet. That, at least, was what she had agreed with the guides to make conversation possible. She took pleasure in it and was relaxed. Obviously she had done this more than once. After a short time the name of my guide was written down. I stared at it: Zoro. 'It can't be the man with the cape?' I asked Elsie, a bit giggly. Luckily that's not what it was; the abbreviation stood for Zoroaster. What a strange way to get into contact with my so-called helpers! I had to find another way of communicating. Spiritualism gives me the creeps and the little table reminded me of it too much. I could no longer ignore that there was 'something', something that really existed though I could not see it. How could I get in contact with this guide myself? I decided to ask 'Zoro' to push my body to the left for a yes, to the right for a no. That at least dispensed with the table. Using this method I got clear answers when I asked clear questions (which is not that easy, especially when you want to ask so many questions with a child-like curiosity about that world there and here). It moved me deeply. Tears streamed down my face at the mere thought that this presence was there for me. And that he had time and attention for the person I really was, just like that, whether I made contact or not. I felt the enormous love with which I was touched, for that is what it was. The odd time when I wanted to know too much, I was pushed backwards very gently, as if to say: take a nice nap, rest a bit now . . . When I asked an unclear question or it was too soon for an answer, he shook me gently.

In the beginning I could barely grasp the unseen and elusive world that was opening up for me. The experiences were surprising, often bewildering. It was incredibly exciting but my palpable, visible little world was being quite thoroughly turned upside down. How do I give all this a place in my daily life? With everything I can touch, smell, taste? And yet I was moved. This really happened. One evening, when I was being rocked as if by an invisible hand, with pure, sweet love, while I sat cross-legged on the bed reading, I phoned my oldest friend Marijke to tell her about it. In a way I wanted to make it even more real for myself by talking out loud about it to someone. Afterwards I demonstrated the wondrous phenomenon to other friends and talked about it enthusiastically.

Another dimension to learn to live in. To allow the invisible into my life, knowing there were beings around me who saw me, felt me and empathised with me. What a treasure! The most beautiful experience I had in my contact with Zoro was probably that evening I was writing a letter by the light of my desk lamp. Tired from working at my desk and partly for fun, actually just like that, I asked Zoro to give my tired body a massage. A bit later I felt a light touch on my left foot. As if somebody was skilfully massaging my foot . . . Strangely enough I continued writing, half my attention on my letter. You simply just can't grasp a thing like that, can you? After a while the full reality of what was happening dawned on me. I put down my pen, my whole attention on the touch now. I closed my eyes to experience and digest what was happening. An invisible hand touched my skin. I could have been frightened but fear didn't belong here, it was too sweet, too gentle for that.

It felt strange and yet very natural just to get up. Would he leave or hang on to my toe? What does one do in such a situation? Oh well, I switched off the light and went upstairs to bed. He was still there and under his touch I fell into a deep and restful sleep.

It was all so new, this relationship with the world of the guides, Zoro, the physical touch, the immense love. Why was Zoro not a man of flesh and blood! It could be the ideal love affair . . . It threw me a bit, yet made me feel so enthusiastic: this was my first tangible experience with the realm beyond the visible, palpable world. Finally!

When Elsie told me she was giving a workshop in England together with Martha, I enrolled in it. At that period of my life she too was a guide for me, a living one. She showed me a path that became a turning point in my life. There in England I worked through the divorce to a large extent and came back extremely open and vulnerable. She had warned me about this and quite rightly so, for all I wanted to do was to go and sit in the woods by the roots of the trees and eat tubers. What came closest were those white tasteless roots, salsify And then, years later, you suddenly read that roots cleanse the liver. Yes, I had had quite a lot on my liver.

On one of those training weekends at the 'Drackenburg Volkshogeshool' I heard about an American woman who could 'read' your colours. The colours of your aura. If there was anything I felt like doing, it was certainly to get to know the colours around me, my own colours. Six months later she had time for me.

Mary she was called, she sat facing me, thin black mid-length hair, round body, her short little legs just reaching the floor; she closed her eyes to see better. A couple of times she asked for my name and then looked straight through me. I learned that 'reading' is indeed literally reading. Through that reading of my energy centres, the chakras and my aura, I was suddenly a lot more than that blonde-haired woman who sat there in front of her in jeans. For from my chakras she could read the lives I seemingly had lived in the past. She told me that I lived in a greater context. That there was a lot more than this life alone. Associations were made, colours seen, past had something to do with present.

'The Tower of the tarot cards stands behind you. I seldom come across that. You have reached a crossroads in your life where you are giving yourself a choice: continuing to comply with the unwritten laws and regulations, the standards of your surroundings, what is expected of you since childhood, or listening to those other parts of yourself which cannot develop within that structure. You have learned a lot from the past, lessons like obeying, putting yourself second, doing your duty, meeting the demands of others, doing your best and trying to live up to the expectations of a lot of people. But what the tarot card indicates is that now you are peeling away the norms and standards you were brought up with in your life. To go your own way. You are making a total change within yourself. You come from a family with a strong tradition which makes it more difficult for you to go your own way. For the change you are undertaking cannot be, is not possible, according to those norms. But you are doing it anyway. You are following the road of your real self and deep down you know it, albeit unconsciously. Therefore the pain you suffer now is bearable because you know that this is your path. In fact, you cannot do otherwise. I see your sorrow. Sorrow for the confusion and pain your change brings about in people around you. Sorrow about saying goodbye to dear ones you leave behind you. Sorrow for the change itself. For the uncertainty of the new, the vulnerability of not knowing how your life will develop from here on.

'Let me tell you, you have the strength for this parting of the ways, for as such it looks like energy. You are enormously creative, the creativity just streams out of your hands. Also intuitive. You too can read people's finer energies, like the aura and the chakras. At any rate you can easily learn how to do it. You have come a long, long way. As a small child you came to earth with the expectation that the world would be 'good'. That people would be warm and sweet. You had formed a whole idea of the world. It soon proved not to fit, and because of your great sensitivity in seeing through things you started to shut yourself off. You built a wall around yourself so as not to get hurt any more. You have been seen and understood so little that you decided to let nobody, or hardly anybody, into your inner circle. You started to adapt to the hypocrisy of the world and you learned to comply with the norms in order to be seen and appreciated. You even gave up your openness to nature; it seems that you found comfort there as a child as an antidote to the lack of authenticity with which 'grown-ups' live . . .'

And Mary went on like that for half an hour. She gave me the craziest details as if she were reading from a book about me. I recognised things but, more important, I became a human being with more dimensions than you think you see before you at first glance! There really is so much more than we can see straight away. Always I had felt and known this and longed for it. I experienced it as a relief, a feeling of great space. As if, because of it, the opportunities in my life had grown. The wider perspective gave more substance to the inevitability of where and how you are born. She told me that I had many lives behind me in which I had been a priestess and someone who relished power and certainly also a voluptuary, in the body of a man or a woman, and that I had learned many facets of life on earth. Ever since, this has helped me to trust my own inner voice more, for it surely meant that I knew a thing or two from my own experience! Not the critical voice that for ever raises its head, not the cynical one, the uncertain one or the angry one, but 'the voice of inner knowing', as a friend of mine used to sing.

For I realised that, just like everyone else with an experienced soul, I had already gone through a great deal.

There is a wall in my room and against that wall I beat my head as hard as I can. Bang, bang, bang. Later I heard they thought that someone was hitting nails into the wall . . .

It becomes more and more apparent that adults say one thing and mean something else.

It scares me. I get attacks of blind anger and climb on the

*high bars of my small wooden bed and bang my head against
the wall with all my might. I don't want the world like that! Not
like that.*

*One evening in my room, in bed, before going to sleep, I
scream at all the grown-ups together. 'There is a lion in my
bed!' Under the blue cover there is a lion, I'm sure of it. The
grown-ups say it is not true. They pull away the covers and
show me their logic. But my reality is different. There is a lion
in my bed.*

*It is spring. The humid air is heavy with promises, with possi-
bilities. She is eleven. She is wearing a light blue dress and sits
in her secret little spot deep in the woods, on the small wood-
en gangplank above the dark water. At each end of the gangplank two bright white birches are standing like her faithful
guardians. Their gossamer branches reaching high up in the
noon sky. Wild long grass grows between their roots, with dots
of yellow and gold of the buttercups and the daisies. The red
withered beech leaves, left over from before the winter, are
lying on top of it and among it. She looks at the reflection of
the trees in the water. Their supple trunks, the leaves that
rustle and tell her about tender things as do the movements
of the water itself. She has taken off her shoe and dips one toe
into the water. Circles ripple out from her toe. The water frowns
and laughs for everything begins to dance on the dark surface.
She looks and listens. For hours. Taking in the colours and the
smells and the rhythm of everything around her. She takes a
deep breath. Here outside she is at home.*

*Here her heartbeat can dance and join in the playful inter-
action of the plants, the swarming insects and the animals, the
trees, the water, the air, the clouds, the sun, the intense humid
smell and growing power of the earth. The harmony is so natural, she is part of it. She draws a deep breath. She knows she
is safe.*

*She gets up and, as she does so often, wanders around.
Touching a leaf here, an unfurling fern there. She lets the fresh*

green leaves of the beech caress her face like the hand of a loved one. Softness and love surround her. Her own face is soft and her heart is wide open to everything around her. To the rays of the sun through the woods. The crystal-clear dew-drops hanging on the cobwebs. She watches intently the spider who is spinning its web. Fascinated she absorbs the patience with which the small creature begins over and over again, the power of that small body, the permanent renewal. She hears the clarity of a bird's song. She sees the bursting bark of the birch and its leaves flickering in the gentle wind of spring. In the deeper woods there are masses of luxuriant ferns. To lie down in, to disappear in. On her belly. Carefully bending back the ferns she sees the dark skin of the earth. Insects crawl around. A small beetle, ants, a ladybird flies out of the dark onto her arm. She turns on her back and looks up into the deep blue sky. She listens to the sounds, the song of life.

When, at school, I get strong migraine attacks, with black spots in front of my eyes, I am not allowed to go home. In the dark school hallway, coats hanging higgledy-piggledy on both walls, the headmistress takes me aside. She is a tall, thin woman. To my eyes she looks old and severe with her grey hair in a small bun and her sharp nose. She bends over me. 'There is no way you can go home just like that. Child, you must know how to persevere in life. You can't just give up your duty for every little pain,' she hisses down at the little child that looks upwards. I feel small and powerless and absolutely do not dare to stand up for myself.

What struck me most after Mary's story was that I could change my life. Over the years I built up my own theory about that, through reading many fascinating philosophies and through the experiences and insights of my own practice as an 'energy-reader' (also called an aura-reader). What Mary had done with me, the reading of my energies, in time I did too. Thereby having one surprise after another. And I still get surprises every day. In fact, surprise has become an integral part of my life. For when during a reading you get in touch with the present-life problems of the person who sits in front of you, every now and then former lives surface that are relevant to the pain, the sickness or questions in the here and now. Your boundaries are constantly altered, for you 'see' things you never could think up yourself. The more past lives I read, the more I wondered how it actually worked. It finally dawned on me that you incarnate on earth to learn from the experiences you get through/in/with/from your body. Materialised, having become matter in flesh and blood, visible, palpable, on this tangible world, earth. With this fascinating but also difficult faculty of thought. With your inner knowing, with feelings you yourself can more or less consciously create. With your choice of possibilities. With your physical condition with its ups and downs. In short: as a human being.

What equally became increasingly clear to me is that you are not lived by something outside of yourself but that you determine your own life. Through your choices, through your characteristics. Couldn't it be, then, that you determine your own birth? With which parents and in what times? In which culture? To me this does seem logical in view of one's own free will.

It may all sound a bit weird but I think you choose to incarnate in the time and place where, firstly, you can learn what you 'haven't had' yet and, secondly, you get a chance to finish what you did not succeed at in former lives or did not complete. Not because a 'higher' power determines it, but from your own choice. What for? I asked myself. I came to a temporary conclusion: because every being plays a part in, is part of the growth of, the primordial source, love, or the light that is in everything. All that is. Not in a static way but during the process of learning, of moving as part of all that lives on this earth, part of the growth, of continuous change. Continuous movement.

Humankind has its own place within this, just like all other life on earth.

A majority of astronomers nowadays assume that there are life forms in several parts of the vast cosmos. It makes sense to me that there, as on earth, the beings, the essences, learn their lessons, and are nurtured by and give nurture to the movement of the whole of the cosmos. It looks like earth is a place where duality is the basis for the human curriculum. Sometimes people say earth is the planet of fear. Which amounts to the same thing, for when there is choice there is fear. Knowing and consciousness.

In the meantime a life has passed. A life of choices and the consequences of those choices. It is a bumpy road to one's own perception. To trust in one's own knowing and thinking. Each time to become a bit more free from my own restrictions, contrary to what I learned as a good girl. To let it slide off me like an old coat that doesn't fit any more, that has been worn out. That isn't something you do without difficulty, for the familiarity of old habits, of deep-rooted frames of reference, of unwritten laws about what is 'good' and what 'should be' is, after all, comfortably safe.

Today my anger has gone. That anger was necessary . . . in order to overcome so much. Dead right, with a lion with claws and huge jaws like that in your bed . . . It is remarkable that the more I had cut myself off from my own intuition, the more I had also cut myself off from nature.

So it was true what Mary had said: learning to read the energies in the chakras and the aura and all the energies around us was indeed part and parcel of my gifts. I discovered this when I attended some courses to satisfy my huge curiosity about looking beyond things. My thirst for knowing and understanding the metaphysical side of life gave me enough motivation to do the course, in which you are expected to look deep inside yourself, and later the whole training. Soon after, I started teaching in the same institute about subtle energies and the possibilities of healing yourself (making yourself 'whole'). I developed new courses about how you are programmed by the culture in which you grow up and how this programming is embedded in you, literally in all your cells. About the extent to which you want to accept this conditioning and what kind of stand you want to take. Following from this, I did all kinds of enjoyable things like giving dance workshops and teaching people to talk with trees. Dancing involves feeling rhythms, getting to know your own rhythm. When your body responds to the tones of a waltz, you make totally different movements from when you let yourself be led by the sounds of Japanese music, for instance. I noticed people making movements they had never made before. It had a kind of alienating effect, yet it gave a new freedom. A step further was communication with trees, which have rhythms completely alien to us. I taught people to feel and perceive those rhythms in all kinds of ways. It had taken me several years to train myself in learning to perceive clearly, in creating space for my intuition and learning to trust it. This ongoing self-examination required more letting go of the old, crying through of sorrow, experiencing and releasing of pain. Freeing myself further from prejudices and judgements. Things I had hitherto found important became less important or disappeared totally from my life. A world of greater insights and associations opened up for me. It lightened up my life and certainly made it more cheerful. As a result I led a more autonomous life, a bit less conformist, and I also had a much broader awareness. And ultimately, due to this wider overview, I had a very strong sense of how everything related to everything else. The layers of consciousness, the relationship of things, the seeing and feeling of the many different subtle energies, the opportunities for change and the wonderful realisation that you can determine your own life. The message that human beings are sinners, the idea of original sin, fatalism, the constricted forms into which we have squeezed 'religion' made it clear for me that all of this has been overly reduced to a 'small, human-sized scale'. For me, at any rate, the actual reality is totally different and in every form of life I perceive the presence of that which we have started to call 'divine'. I now prefer to call it 'light'. All of this light here on earth is, I think, a part of the primordial source, the generator of that light.

I read about a theoretical physicist, Dr Fritz Albert Popp*, who in 1974 made the exciting discovery that there is 'life light' in the gherkin. I quote: 'With sensitive apparatus he could measure the light radiated by the gherkins.' In his research he went further and found that 'there is light in the cells of all living beings, from the gherkin up to and including man'. He gave these light particles the name 'biophotons' for in physics the smallest light particles are called photons.

He further discovered that biophotons are carriers of information. To quote further: '. . . they see to it that in a plant, as in other organisms, equally in man, every single cell simultaneously knows everything that happens in the organism (. . .) The radiation of the biophotons comes from the DNA which is present in all cells (. . .) Not like a small lightbulb but like a small laser beam! (. . .) Because of their physical properties laser beams are simultaneously information-beams (. . .) What man only recently has started to apply, nature has used in a perfected form since primordial times. The laser show of nature implies the transference of an incredible amount of information at the speed of light, both within the organism and mutually between organisms for they do not limit themselves to the organism but reach other organisms as well (. . .) From unicellular ones through flowers and animals up to and including man (. . .) without man (. . .) perceiving (consciously) *this all-encompassing form of communication.*' Popp and a great many other scientists are thus measuring the light of life itself!

What I myself discovered is that when you direct your conscious attention to a stone or a flower or whatever form of life, the light in that stone shines more brightly for the energy grows through that directed attention. This means that with

* See: Dagny Kerner, Imre Kerner, *De taal van de plant (The language of the plant)*, Ankh-Hermes, Deventer

real attention everything comes to more radiating, more powerful life. Just try it! The light that we humans have in *all* our
cells we too can make brighter in each other and in ourselves.
When the attention is non-judgemental, open to the life in the
other, without expectations, that light gets more of a chance.

These discoveries were for me a confirmation of my own
completely unscientific findings! Really very exciting . . .

The training took me back to my own original knowing
which, in one way or another, contains more light than knowledge. Knowledge I had amassed in school, from books, via
many teachers, my parents and my surroundings. What I
learned had crowded out my own intuition and had made me
uncertain about my own feelings and thoughts. It seems like
the whole educational system is geared towards that. You
receive lots of useful information to enable you to do something in our society. Your knowledge, what you have learned,
is to a great extent your support. It is considered essential. But
your knowing, what you already have as a child or still have
because you bring it with you from former experiences, that
gets little or no confirmation, stimulation or appreciation!
Knowing is something totally different from the knowledge you
gather and serves another purpose. It leads you along other
roads.

You need your knowing to survive in emergencies and to
make choices in your life. In a moment of knowing you are in
a different part of your body than when you are using knowledge *about* something. It is situated higher, right above your
head or in your heart or in your belly. Knowledge-about sits in
your head. It gives you a headache sometimes. Your knowing
stands, as it were, above knowledge-about. It is clearer. In my
experience you are then in the territory of soul-knowing. The
knowing you have acquired over lifetimes. I think that you function at your best when knowledge and knowing work together and are integrated. Do you know the feeling you get when
you read a 'thinking-book' that excites you? You are excited
for the precise reason that you know what it says is true
because you know it already. As such there is a lot of know-

ing inside you that is to some extent dormant but can wake up at the craziest moments. Meditation and inner perception can be of help with this. But equally a remark made by somebody or an image you see somewhere. Is truth ever Truth or is it no more than the truth of the moment? The instant you pin it down it can become dogmatic and as such it limits your freedom. The truth of your own inner knowing sometimes pops up out of and through what came before. It stands on its own and is not static. Only connected to the circumstances of the true reality of the moment. That is free perception.

We are a long way from the invisible. Really it means we have lost respect for the essence of things. In his book *Rebirth of Nature* Rupert Sheldrake shows us how, via the humanist reformation, we have ended up with 'the disenchantment of the world' as he puts it so well. The mechanistic world has replaced the wondrous.

We are like orphans, cut loose from the magical power inherent in everything. We are no longer connected. Not with the endless stories and experiences of objects, nor with the powers of nature, nor with each other as human beings, nor with each other's cultures, nor with the elements, Mother Earth, the plant world, the natural world, the spirit world, nor with animals. We are more connected with the ever-present noise around us, the asphalt on the roads and the confusing, often destructive messages that intrude on us via television. Where is it ever quiet? The day starts and ends with radio and television news. Yes, at four o'clock in the morning you can still hear the birds, almost without background noise. The violence of noise has become natural, the stench we no longer smell. The head is the most valued part of our body, and within that head our brain takes pride of place. It does overtime and for this we compensate by cramming ourselves full of any kind of food or by over-emphasising sport and sex. We are cut off from that light in ourselves. Crazily enough we do not even live at all in the consciousness of our body, our 'I'. We force our body to extremes. It is more like an enemy we berate continuously when it raises its voice. Where did I forget how to be connected to the natural elements in a natural way, with my whole body and all my senses, with my whole self, with the possibility of wonder? What happened to us that we no longer see nature and the natural world as a partner of equal value in the game of life on earth? Why am I not fully alive to the fact that as a human being I cannot live without all that grows on the earth, without all the layers beneath it with all the riches it contains and the animals that connect the various elements? When did we stop respecting the natural world? Why did we not learn as children that all our food comes from the earth? Why was there no talk about that? Was it so far removed from the dining table and daily reality? Was it that ordinary that it wasn't appreciated or even seen any more?

We no longer stop to think that this small calf was specially bred and slaughtered just for us and now lies on the shelves cut up into little bits, wrapped in plastic, to be thrown carelessly into a supermarket trolley and eaten unthinkingly one evening.

When Martha tells me that the earth will soon explode, as if to shake off all our pollution and all our mistakes, I think: that would not surprise me. All the Marthas of the world, you are right. I know nothing about the oh so sensitive world out there, outside my house, my town, my comforts. Nothing, and I wouldn't know what to do with it anyway. I am a stranger in the presence of my original mother, the earth. Cut off.

I have to take better care of the environment they say. Yes, but I haven't the slightest clue what it is! Environment sounds and feels like 'a thing', without life. How can I identify with 'a thing'? When I don't feel connected with it, it's no wonder I surreptitiously put bottles out with the garbage if I'm too lazy to drive to the glass container with my stinking exhaust.

I have no idea how to deal with flowers, trees, vegetables or animals. Actually I'm afraid of all that unknown life. Not only of the cows when I want to cross their pasture. Their big eyes look at me so vaguely that I think that any moment I could be tossed by the ladies' horns or trampled under a hoof. I have literally lost all my intuition about the natural world. Once upon a time, even we Westerners must have known what and when to plant and which herbs to use when. What is good for you and when, and when not.

Did science obscure all our natural knowing? Are the big syrupy lumps of knowledge that we have let into our brains from the books of 'those-who-know' so dominating that we think we don't know the most ordinary things any more? It is all too crazy that we women consult handbooks about how to take care of a baby. I become very uncertain of my own ideas when one of these 'ones-who-know' tells me how it has to be done. As a child nobody taught me that I can also know things simply by listening to my intuition! Somebody at least could have taught me that I myself know lots of things.

Another earwig carelessly tossed down the drain, with a jet of water so that the little animal slides down extra deep. I don't do that to give earwig number umpteen a gentle death with the excuse that it probably survives better in water; no, I want it gone. Gone.

I am getting a bit fed up with continually picking up spiders and earwigs in bits of kitchen roll and shaking them neatly out of the window. Actually quite wonderful (despite feelings of guilt) to kill one every now and then! That whole sweet charade, it makes me sick!

I am tired, intensely tired. My head is full and my body feels really heavy. As if I am being pulled downwards. Tired. A fortnight in the mountains to recover from working hard in two full jobs, from children, problems, people, busy-ness and moving house. From thinking-of and caring-for.

After a journey on a crowded and endless motorway we arrive in pastures full of flowers, the quietness of dark-green woods and above them powerful giants of grey granite and limestone topped here and there with a piece of eternity. White. Wider than ever, gigantic.

Below in the valley, here and there a tiny village. No people.

No people and silence. I breathe in the thin air deeply.

Arms stretched upwards. Slowly letting the air penetrate my midriff and between and behind all my ribs.

Moved by so much beauty, I doubt whether I can handle this splendour. One day of getting used to it, carefully. Listening. Listening to the river that cuts through the valley far below and the rest is silence. Days later, acclimatised in body and soul to my natural surroundings, I walk through the immense forests. Thus falls the first small barrier between me and nature. Moss hangs in crotchety threads from the spruces. It is cool and humid under the trees. I climb over stones up the mountainside and go and sit with my back against a sturdy fir. Eyes closed, sunlight through the branches on my face. Listening, breathing, feeling. How I love this piece of land.

Slowly I let everything in: the deep blue sky in which you could drown, dissolve, lose yourself if you look at it long enough. Endless.

The tops of the spruces and the larches that, bolt upright, provide a contrast of dark and light green against all that blue. In between and above all of that, the rocks which create steep walls and bottomless abysses in fantastic chunks and restful planes. Colours grey, brown, ochre, and black seams.

Birds of all sizes come and go, playfully certain of their goal.

In the midst of all that life I sit. I try to play along. But painfully I feel the distance created by cities and prosperity that makes an open encounter impossible. I am sitting on the earth amidst crawling, frolicking, sparkling life and as a human being cannot talk with it. And it cannot talk with me. Yet I feel the movement in all things, around things as well. The rhythms, the vibrations. It is the emanation of all the different animals and plants and trees that I perceive. The perception in itself is the beginning of a dialogue . . . If I my perception were improved, couldn't I communicate better as well?

It makes me think of the atmosphere you sense when you walk into a room full of people, at a birthday party for instance, and you feel immediately whether that atmosphere is agreeable to you or not. Just like when you walk into the woods and the atmosphere of those woods feels good to you in that moment or it does not. That atmosphere is the energy the woods, or the group of people at the birthday party, radiate. The spot in which I am sitting feels good, safe and quiet; it clearly has a nice energy for me in this moment. With just one individual on their own you sense the emanation, the energy, even more strongly. When somebody is sad or angry or feels good, they involuntarily radiate that energy, often without knowing it. And in that moment it feels fine to you, or not, for it can be healing, fulfilling, loving or exactly the opposite. You feel better with one tree than with another because the energy that tree radiates does or does not add something. Everybody can sense that. It only takes a willingness to be open to it and a certain peace of mind to perceive it consciously. From there it is only a small step to learn to listen to the vibrations. Communication with the natural world is possible, just like unspoken contact with a loved one. In this you can sense whether he or she is cross or is relaxed and contented.

A couple of years ago I read a book written by a woman, *Behaving As If the God in All Life Mattered.** That book now helps me to believe in what I sense and see. She relates how she developed a strong and purposeful exchange with plants and how she made her vegetable garden 'in consultation' with the nature beings.

I have a great need for some kind of communication with my surroundings and I am teaching myself to open up more and more to the energies. Thus I hear, see and sense more. I notice that when I concentrate fully, I can penetrate to the heart of a plant and then, as it were, grasp its frequency. Afterwards I have to pull myself out of it very clearly before I can perceive

---

* Machaelle Small Wright, *Behaving As If the God in All Life Mattered*, Perelandra, 1983, 1987.

something else or simply look at that blue sky. If I don't, I notice everything gets blurred and runs into each other. As if I need an eraser to be able to see and sense 'cleanly' again. I can't keep up this kind of openness for too long or I get the same effect. But how do I keep the communication open? Daily life will gobble me up in a minute. There are two different worlds, that of humans and that of nature, one that plays indoors and one outside. We don't know each other any more.

It takes time. Time. The elements of nature have endless patience, they are ready for an open dialogue. Not only do our housing and living habits stand in the way, but our fears and uncertainties as well. Our would-be certainties. To let those go is very difficult indeed. Opening your heart to the unconditional love of the natural world often evokes resistance for it is not for nothing that you closed your heart during the course of your life. There is pain in that heart and it often caused you to close down emotionally. 'I'm fine' is safer than showing the sorrow, the hurt, and experiencing it is the last thing you want to do. The pain is long gone, you think. The door has been closed. And you don't think about it, that the pain, the sorrow, that has not yet been worked through, sits like a lump somewhere in your body. With our closed doors our external image becomes more important than the inner life that we experience only partially. Here in the West we judge each other by our achievements, our prestige, our possessions and money, our attainments in the field of science, our expertise or our skill in this or that field. All those things are valued and thus we hardly let our real self be seen, only now and then by one or two people. And with each disappointment in work and relationship we close our little doors a bit more. That is a formidable barrier to starting a meaningful dialogue with anyone or anything. Because nature does not communicate with words, it asks you to communicate through your feelings, so we have a problem here.

That night a crashing thunderstorm erupts over the giants that surround us. Lightning standing out brightly against the ink-black air. The wind gusts strongly around the house. We just manage to get wood inside without getting soaked. We light the fire. Relishing it. Indoors a little nest is quickly made. Warm and cosy. Outside lightning flashes. That night again I feel how safe this house is for me. A small landslide could be the only danger here. In fact, I should insure myself against it. We sleep like roses for a whole ten hours.

The next morning I call the insurance man. 'No, madam, not in Switzerland.' That same night there had been a landslide in the valley below. It had engulfed everything. A real catastrophe. Houses had been destroyed, trains could no longer run because of the tons of mud everywhere. We didn't notice a thing! Only felt the possibility of it and from our little nest simply enjoyed a brilliant thunderstorm. Can you enjoy yourself while around the corner dramas are unfolding, natural disasters are wreaking destruction and claiming victims? War, hunger, disease? 'You are not free as long as somebody is suffering,' they said during my political period. Is that really so?

The mountain stream ripples gently and steadily. An age-old spot. Here too wisdom is present in trees, rocks, water. The sun has almost set behind the mountains on the other side of the valley. It is making a purple-black wall with long bundles of sunbeams over the ridges of the rocks. I watch it from the meadow opposite where I sit high up in the last of the sunlight. I walk over to my friend the old larch. Just to say hallo and see how she is doing. She stands there sprawling and offers motherly protection to all life beneath her sturdy branches. While I stand against her I ask her about somebody who has come into my life. Aloud I say: 'I don't know what to do with it,' and I hear: 'Let him go. Learn to love people, just like that, without wanting something with them. Enjoy a person and look at them, experience them.' An answer! Is this autosuggestion? But where then does this clear answer come from? She, the tree, has no mouth through which she can formulate words with air and vocal cords. How does this work? I didn't say those words and there is not a living soul around. Remarkably the words of the answer formulated themselves not in my head but inside of me. They came out of my chest, my heart chakra. The larch and I can talk together then, have a conversation . . . Her vibrations form themselves into words.

In awe I try to 'talk' with her once more. I ask a question but this time nothing happens. I take a few steps backwards to see her in her entirety and only now it strikes me how frail she looks. This tree who radiates so much tranquillity and space seems to be suffering from acid rain. Her needles are hanging listlessly downwards. It looks as if she has lost heart. Damn it, how sad. I don't want this. It makes me furious. How can we make such a complete mess of it? Is there some way we can share the earth fairly? Love it? There are sweet spots on television, little films, information. But I don't think this will be enough and I ask myself whether this is the way. People ought to get directly in touch with nature again. But how? Through feeling? Talking? Now that I know it's feasible, totally new possibilities open up. Trees are obviously wise beings with old souls we can share our worries with and ask for advice, and who can indicate to us what is and is not good for them. What do they need from us? Good heavens, what a lot we have to learn from each other. I know somebody who says the world will explode. Is it irrevocable?

Wandering like this through the woods and the higher alpine meadows, I notice that this summer an essential boundary between me and that other life around me has disappeared. It seems that I can perceive at a deeper dimension. Firstly I feel and hear how everything vibrates. Then the conversation with the larch. I see colours more intensely because I can look more deeply into them, as it were. As if the colour lets me in at that depth. In this moment I feel thin and vulnerable, the wind could pick me up just like that. A resistance has gone, and so I am receptive to the most subtle energies of the plants and flowers, the trees, the wind, the mountains. There is no longer a barrier between all that life and me. There is a direct contact for I am suddenly open to the subtlest energies. Colours, vibrations, smells. Something very gentle. How has this happened all at once? Am I so tired that my boundaries are gone? My human distance? Is this really possible?

It seems as if everything communicates with everything else and now I am beginning to be part of that! It is so simple, so direct and so real. And above all it is so true. I feel like touching everything, feeling everything with my hands and my lips, my skin. I want to suck up the smells of the juniper berries, the spruces, the stones in the sun, the smallest flowers, the early-morning dew, the cow manure. That is part of it too. Everywhere I see small marmots, having emerged from their hiding places, standing like little guardians with their heads in the wind. What is happening with me? Love for everything washes over me and tenderness surges through me.

It is about something entirely different from human communication. It goes deeper than words and gestures can ever convey. There is something limitless in it as well, maybe because it is not about doing but about being. For one or another reason it seems to be a very old and yet very delicate 'beingness'.

These are days of magical moments and powerful emotion. A new way of life opens up for me. One afternoon I am called by something outside. I don't know what it is but I go and have a look. Good heavens: out there the sun is shining, I am standing in the middle of it, to my right hardly one metre away I see the rain coming down very gently and to my left stands a rainbow in full glory, powerfully radiating its colours over the whole width of the immense valley. I have to breathe deeply a couple of times to be able to take it all in. It is as if in this moment anything can happen, as if anything is possible, anything. Never before have I experienced space so intensely. I feel free, free. Open to everything around me. And I danced, danced in the rain, in the sun, and in a piece of rainbow.

And then my diary told me I had to go home, too soon to digest all of this. Too soon to be able to close myself off a bit before I plunged once again into the violence of our Western society. I remained open and vulnerable. Full of wonder, full of something I had never known in that way before and that spoke to deeper levels than ever in myself and opened up new, unknown possibilities for me.

At home responsibilities awaited me. The clutter and busyness of the Netherlands. For the first time it struck me how little space there is in our country for nature itself. I looked like crazy for quiet places in the woods and fields but always I found people, people with dogs, or dirty scraps of paper, cans, torn and trampled branches. Everywhere the visible presence of people. Nowhere inviolate space, nowhere real silence. The voice of the bird was never contained in silence. Always there was the sound of a train, the screech of a jet flying over, the dull background noise of traffic in the distance. Suddenly the pressure of my work became unbearable, the time pressure oppressive, and I couldn't muster the concentration necessary for my job. I couldn't concentrate at all, nothing worked any more, I couldn't take it any longer.

Each time I enter the building where I work I develop a pressure on my head and, once at work, a woolly heaviness settles over my whole head. It feels like a kind of hood that makes it very difficult to keep my attention focused. It is with utter difficulty that I keep my eyes open and I do my utmost not to show it. Naturally that only half works for we know each other too well. What I most would like to . . .

My little voice of Duty says: 'You can't do that! You have your responsibilities. You can't let your friends down. When you start something you must complete it.' 'Oh dear,' says my little Inside voice, 'I'm so tired . . . I can't go on any longer. I would rather go and lie down.' 'You can't do that.' 'No, I can't,' I sigh and I try to shove off the hood that is over my head. It doesn't work of course. A week later the hood is already there when I get into my car at home to go to work. What should I do?

'You really ought to stop work for three months,' says a

friend at the end of a 'reading'. The first one to jump up is the indignant little voice of Duty. Imagine, three months . . . And what about your responsibilities then?' 'Yes,' sighs my little Inside voice, 'you are right.'

A week later, a colleague sees me at my work, sits down and says: 'You should stop work for three months, starting now.' I look at her with big eyes. This is too crazy, she is saying exactly the same thing! 'Well, yes, it simply isn't possible now and certainly not just like that. The season is just starting, there is so much work . . .' 'Of course it's possible and right away even. I take over the first couple of tasks from you and you go home now, you have a long bath or go for a walk, do something nice.' I think I looked at her with the same big eyes for a long, long while, all the little voices in me silenced by fright, and then two tears trickled down my cheeks. Gratitude was the main emotion in that moment. For the attention, the picking up of my immediate tasks just like that. I was being seen. I hardly had to explain it to my co-workers, they had already sensed it and they let me go with great love. With the hefty task of taking over my part of the work.

The three months became a year and I didn't go back to working full days. For my colleagues it wasn't easy, nor for me, but in a different way. It was a year in which I had to sleep away all the tiredness in my body and in which I learned a lot. About myself, about the place work takes in your life and about all that you disregard because of that. Not to work any longer! It took me almost three quarters of a year to get over my tiredness. To get used to a lack of structure. The absence of the fixed framework of a full diary. For all these years I had planned every quarter of every hour, divided my time as best I could between my two jobs and my four children and all that comes with it. And now . . . I was no longer expected; I missed my nice, inspiring colleagues. Who was I really? It was crazy that up until then, as a female professional, I always had been somebody. Even in social contacts outside the job you are that professional. You speak from that position, you think from it, you read the newspaper with working-thinking-eyes, everything.

How did people perceive me now? As what, as who? I had become a professional to be a human amongst other humans, to get close to people, to share and to understand. Earlier on in my life I was seen as the little princess, later as the 'wife of'. And how about now? Presumably everybody who doesn't work or no longer works goes through this. I felt ashamed, empty, useless, ridiculously luxurious just being home all the time. Sometimes I imagined hearing people say: 'That one hasn't got anything better to do . . .' Fears came up, about the lack of structure not only in my day but also in my life. Having to fill the days myself, to make them meaningful, was not an easy task. Afraid. In this world you have to be useful, don't you? And then I was being asked: 'How is your work?' 'What are you doing?' Well . . . I . . . er . . . have taken a sabbatical to . . . er . . . work something out. A project. 'That at least sounds interesting,' said my little Shame-voice.

Doing nothing, that is not allowed. Being useful. A full diary. Occupying yourself with meaningful things. Making a contribution. That gives you a good feeling. You belong. But with a safe barricade of professional knowledge between everyone else and me.

Now I am who I am. Look, this is me then. This is it. Nobody expects me, nothing is expected from me. I myself shall have to give the day structure. I myself shall have to make judgements about myself. Every day. Luckily I meet enough people, children and friends; if not I would only run into myself every day. Now that I was in any case engaged in this process of release, it wasn't such a crazy idea also to experience for once to what extent I could let go of all structures. So I had to be all alone, then, for a few months in a spot where I know nobody and nobody knows me. A need for silence and being away from all that is familiar — work, people, image, reputation, being a woman — helped me to make this decision. I encountered no one but myself, through all those days. I wasn't always good company. And yet this is what I wanted to experience. I felt it was necessary even though I didn't quite know why. The first few weeks were hard and painful. Many days I didn't feel at all like meeting myself. I could think of more enjoyable things to do. The contact I had experienced with nature a couple of months earlier was different now, less open. I was alone and lonely. Days, weeks, months on end. But all through the silence of loneliness I started to enjoy it more and more. I bought artist's materials and went out into nature. A kind of relationship developed. The concentration necessary to transfer what I saw onto paper filled my day and created the presence of something else as well. The colours, rhythms, smells, the apparent silence of the trees, the rustling of the bushes, the grass, the flowers, the skies, the clouds, the rocks, the earth, the insects, the birds — good heavens! what life, what presence. Now, in the silence of aloneness, all of this got a chance to grow, bit by bit, into a real relationship. One of to and fro, of give and take. Mutual. Something of the original exultant feeling anchored in reality.

I broke through the structure of the daily schedule by painting till the early-morning hours, Mahler's Sixth Symphony in my ears. Rising before dawn to witness the first daylight outside, sitting on a rock close to my beloved larch in the mountain meadow where chamois and deer often come to graze and nibble at the branches and flowers. A thermos with hot tea by my side. New experiences that bring me closer to myself and my surroundings. On the last evening I sit by the open fire with candles around me, so contented that I even take the phone off the hook for fear somebody will disturb my peace.

On the way back two wondrous things happened. I was driving through Belgium on the motorway near Sint-Job-in-het-Goor. I had been driving for hours and was starting to get tired. I was thoroughly sore from sitting, dazed and fatigued. Aloud and casually I asked the sun to give me a helping hand. I was driving at 180 (km.p.h.), shame on me, and was taking a slight curve to the left with the road when I felt with absolute certainty that in that moment I could have let go of the steering wheel because 'something' or 'somebody' could take over from me, and I heard literally: 'Have a rest.' It is baffling to feel the protection around me. This time I heard the voice in exactly the same spot in my body, again in my chest. The same kind of love as with Zoro surrounded me, like the presence of a caring spirit. A warm glow of recognition and trust flowed through my body. I stretched and relaxed.

Close to home something else happened. The sun was setting with beautiful warm, orange rays. There seemed no end to it. The very last ones kept on shining into the sky. I could see it from the corner of my left eye and it was so beautiful that I left the road to see the full light. I stopped the car with its nose pointed towards the sun and watched. It seemed as if that last ray remained hanging there specially to be seen. It was so incredibly beautiful tears came to my eyes. An overpowering need to talk with the sun made me say aloud how much I loved her. My heart ached from loving so much and I felt how that sunbeam reached for me, touched me and moved me. I heard myself saying: 'I never want to be alone again, sun, never again, never again . . . I have had such pain, such terrible pain, I don't want this any more.' The pain of the sorrow and the joy were almost too much for my relatively small body. I wanted to burst, so moved did I feel. A kind of comfort came to me from that one beam, deep into my heart. And I thought I heard: 'That is not necessary, that doesn't have to be.' I was filled with such joy that everything sparkled and shone. And in that state I arrived home soon after. To my children I said simply that I had had an excellent journey.

The sun is shining, the crickets are singing and I still don't know why we are so removed from nature here (this is the only part of the world I am entitled to talk about). I know, from my own experience now as well, what has come between us but why did we let this happen? There's a great difference between walking in the woods and the fields enjoying everything around you and having a dialogue with the elements of nature. That much has become clear to me this year. It is another thing still when you take care of plants and vegetables with your hands in the earth. Walking is a kind of visiting. You walk on the earth

and you see things from the outside. A distance remains: ..
and me. That's the way I experience it anyway. I watch and
enjoy and all the while I am busy with my own numerous
thoughts. In itself it is a very pleasant experience indeed!

Having a dialogue is a deeper dimension. It asks in particular for a mutuality. A willingness and ability to listen and perceive. Equally it requires an openness to surprise, for the
instances you get to see or the words you hear are always unpre-
dictable. You are no longer the protagonist nor are you anything
less. You are together. And you have a lot to tell each other and
a lot to give, from different starting points, for you are different
from each other. For some this may come very naturally. For
me this wider awareness was something I had to attain. As a
child I frisked my way through the colours. Through all the experiences in my life I arrived at this awareness.

As far as working with the earth is concerned, I don't know
enough about that, alas. Probably because in our society I have
not been taught to listen to my own intuition, I am always hes-
itant about what can or cannot be done in working the earth.
I can only go by what I have read and heard and when you
are working with the earth you often have no contact at all with
what you are touching. Then you remain the superior human,
as it were, master of the plants. Plants are there for humans.
Without us plants could not grow. And that kind of nonsense.
Yes, when you take plants inside you have to take care of them.
But outside, there everything grows without you. Maybe not
exactly the way you want it to, but it still grows.

Currently I have not been working within a fixed framework
for about a year, I no longer have two full jobs and my youngest
child is about to leave home. In the meantime I know I have
stepped out of the hustle and bustle of my work because I
needed the time, and in our society this means the tranquillity, to access unknown forms of communication in my search
for the essence of the cosmos and all that exists in that unfathomable space. That immediately made my working-world set-
up unbearable. The two ways of being collided with each other.
One in constant tension, with me caught up in responsibilities

I had enthusiastically taken on, alongside the lightness and playfulness of the other reality: my new friends. The encounter with that whole natural world was so intense that, just as when one falls in love, I couldn't put distance between the tree and myself. I wanted to be part of it all and would have liked to go and lie down in the greenery and remain lying there. Still and close. With all my pores wide open to the lavender in front of my nose, the spruce, the grass. Uninhibited, unlimited surrender. And with it came a feeling of guilt as heavy as lead: that I am human, part of the destruction, that I didn't see, didn't understand. Shame, to have lived alongside this limitless love, thinking about a lot of fairly useless, although often pleasant, things. I go round in vicious circles of guilt and shame. Because I am part of the human race that destroys. That hacks, cuts, pollutes, destroys the nature energies that are becoming more and more familiar to me. Without thinking of the life that is being injured and the feelings of that life. Yes, the feelings.* With disgusting greed and blind ignorance of the harmony and precarious balance of things. Wanting and having. Nature? Go on, nature doesn't feel, isn't conscious, it's light-years inferior to us humans.

Sorrow burns deep in my whole body. Small, minute, I feel next to the grandeur and primordial wisdom of the natural elements.

My heart is heavy, torn by my awareness of the intense undivided love that is everywhere around us humans and which we can live with consciously, and the human duality through which I cut myself off from that love. I am human and I take part in the pollution, the destruction.

I am cut up by it.

What I have brought about, I do to myself. I am desperate and rudderless. How do I deal with this new awareness? It is either/or. Either I become part of nature without any reservations. I feel the flower, the tree, the energy of it, the essence,

---

* See: Peter Tompkins/Christopher Bird, *The Secret Life of Plants*. Penguin, London, 1975.

the emanation that has a certain power. Sometimes it is giggly and cheerful, sometimes strong and positive, sometimes . . .

Or I am cut off from it. Another type of being, gloomy and guilty and feeling worthless. How do I deal with the split, with my own duality? Too vulnerable I withdrew then from all I was doing, knowing it no longer had a place in my world. The only thing left was my total trust that what I was doing was good for me and an inevitable consequence of my choices. The two realities or two levels: that of being and that of doing. I became more and more aware of the poignant difference between the world of 'doing', characteristic of people in our Western society, and that other world of 'being', in which nature lives. So aware indeed that the question of whether I could still actually live in this world inevitably forced itself on me. A world where everything seems to revolve around who we are *not*, but have to be to please other people. If it isn't your parents then there is always somebody who functions as an extension of your parents and whose demands you are trying to meet. Or just the opposite, which amounts to the same thing. And you are convinced that you have to be like this and not otherwise. A world where there is so very little respect for each other and even less for the life of nature. A world where nature has no right to speak out. Nor what is natural in ourselves.

Wouldn't it be a lot more wonderful to flow into that unconditional love? That love that exists in a reality of non-duality, non-differentiated good and bad, the judgement-free part of life on this earth. Free of judgement. A love that is connected with all life, light, the primordial source? Letting myself flow away in that? How could I go on living in this terrible world now that I had got to know this enormous love? I felt sharply what it meant to be a human being who cannot help but vacillate between the two poles of good and bad. And all the gradations in between. With the choices we continually have to make in order to live and to survive. Full of judgement and fear. Always at war with our boundaries, limitations and powerlessness. With our contradictions. Always caught up in what we were doing yesterday and what we have to do tomorrow.

Seldom at the still point of the now. To be human with our sorrow, our yearning, the desire for destruction and power, the pain. The ugliness of which we are capable.

The understanding and intense experience of the power that emanates from judgement-free love threw my knowledge of the complexity of being human into stark contrast. Stark contrast! The light of love made the shadows bigger.

Never before had I come so dramatically into contact with the extremes of duality. I couldn't stand it any longer. The contradiction within myself was unbearable. There was no getting away from it, I felt myself slipping down into a bottomless pit where all the misery of the world seemed to be lumped together. I belonged to it for I am human. What happened then was remarkable for it was unknown to me: I fell into a real depression. Every morning I woke up with a feeling of utter hopelessness. And I went to bed with it. And sorrow, sorrow and more sorrow. About the world, life, the earth, my part in it, my life. The human world with its destruction, filthy violence, lies and hypocrisy, its inequality, searching and drudgery. The wounds of broken relationships, disappointments, lack of respect on all fronts. The seemingly endless wickedness of the world of which I am a part and in which everything seems to be sacrificed to progress. What progress for heaven's sake? Oh why, why . . . ?

Somewhere in the back of my head I knew I would come through this, that this was a kind of death from which new life springs. Meanwhile, despite all I was going through, I continued to have total and complete trust in the meaning of everything. But a helping hand would not be a bad idea. My own ugliness, my part in the destruction of the earth I wanted to look in the eye and process.

On a sunny late-summer morning I go and stand in front of a soft white fully open rose and ask her for forgiveness. I know I am not the whole of humankind and that forgiving will not change inherent human nature but still . . . I need this. I want to say my bit to the whole and I give free rein to all my emotions. She beams at me. And again I feel no separation, we are one. I sort of disappear in her. As balm to the wound of my debt to her, to all of life. Part of the atrocious atrocity. Like this, together as one, for a while I don't feel so much the separate human. For days I approach now the acacia, then the birch, a fragrant pink rose, an apple tree, to be one with them.

Just until I begin to understand that I too as a human being form an essential part of the whole. That it is useless to feel guilty and inferior, for it doesn't make any positive contribution. The capacities in nature, in humans and in the elements are, I think, meant to cooperate, one being just as important as another. In the vast interplay, the different starting points themselves constitute unique contributions that have not come into being for nothing. Precisely the various tasks of the human and the plant and animal worlds contribute not only to life on earth but equally to the growth of the all-encompassing cosmos. Each with its own speciality. Exactly as the differences in world cultures contribute to the development of our humanity.

Now that I understand this I hear and see things that are new or unexpected for me. I play the role of curious co-inhabitant of the cosmic whole which has the delightful advantage that I am not responsible for the so-called survival of the plant world but receive love and wise lessons, nourishment I very much need. It is the juice of my life. Then, one day, I take a completely different stance in relation to that rose: just me, and the rose there as something else, its own self. I no longer have to lose myself in her. We are free of each other and yet one, bound together in freedom. Guilt starts to give way to power. The rose is able to do things I cannot, such as simply being beautiful, loving selflessly and smelling incredibly good. The rose always and only lives in the present moment, knowing no yesterday, no tomorrow. She has feelings (proved by all kinds of tests) but is unable to judge. With the non-existence of duality, of choice, judgement disappears. There is only love. Feeling without judgement. You are never, ever judged by anything in nature. And yet every part of it knows our pain and sympathises with our grief, in the now. I, on the other hand, can think and choose, I will probably never be completely free of judgement, I can move and she cannot. I know fear, and my pain is inextricably connected with past and future. My task is probably more difficult because of my thinking capacity, my choices between making and breaking. But because of this I as a human being have unfathomable creative potential.

My sensitivity becomes more manageable now that I have again given myself a position of full value. That is my starting point for an equal dialogue with nature and all the life forms it embraces. With the consequence that henceforward I conduct my life and work with an attitude of deep respect for all life. Work and space for quiet have found a balance. Fortunately for me it didn't become an either/or choice, but a matter of both being in the world working and being in contact with the subtle language of all that lives. I now knew from the inside out not only that people can learn an incredible amount from each other cross-culturally but also that all that lives on this earth communicates with everything else and has to learn from those others, and that the natural world misses the natural connection that is contact with us humans. It is just lying (and flying and standing and swimming and walking and crawling) there and waiting for us.

In that year of deep valleys and new insights, in the midst of the big, black hole in the middle — weird to be in a dark hole and know you are going to get out of it before long — I thought of Martha, a psychologist. She wasn't involved in my daily life, she was competent, I could trust her. I knew this from the workshop of hers I had done. And so I left for the United States, to visit an old woman who helps people cross thresholds in their process of growth.

3. A Choice

How can one begin to overcome the Eeyore Within, and
thereby begin to counteract the Eeyore Effect? We will go to
that in a moment, but first . . .

Benjamin Hoff, *The Te of Piglet*

It is six o'clock in the morning, European time, when I arrive
out of the cold into a warm kitchen. Fifteen hours I have been
on my way to look up Martha Kilby. This woman, in whose
workshop in England I and fifty other people had experienced
full of admiration how we could work through blockages that
kept us from living. She taught us that it is better to get rid of
your painful stuff during your lifetime than to die with it. That
the transition to death can thus become a passage. It had been
a profound experience and over the following years Martha
and I became closer and closer. The long wooden table is full
with home-made jam and cookies, colourful tins and flowers.
The heat comes out of a big old-fashioned iron stove on legs
that has little doors through which you push logs to feed the
fire. Untidy lists of phone numbers and little notes hang next
to the wall phone. A stub of pencil dangles from a piece of
string beside it. Dark-reddish wooden walls and benches surround the jolly table. Small windows through which you can
see the night outside. It is twelve o'clock American time. 'And
tell me now why you have come,' my hostess says. These are
the last days of the year and her only free week. She is alone,
she has time. She knows from my letter that I want to process

old undigested parts of my life. She knows too that this has to do with a phase in my life in which I am re-evaluating everything. Good heavens, where do I start? Stupefied by the journey, at the other side of the world with a woman I haven't seen in years, this question comes at me too directly for my dazed head. Where is the essence of my journey?

'It's a long story, Martha. It started during my last holiday in the mountains of Switzerland in the summer. I was really dead tired but barely aware of it. I had two great jobs that I fully dedicated myself to with all my enthusiasm and creativity, and which carried their attendant responsibilities. On top of that, all my four children were going through their puberty years at the same time and presented me with quite a lot of challenges. But I didn't feel that I needed a vacation. Everything was going very well. Every moment of the day was occupied and made good use of. As a single parent all the responsibilities fall on my shoulders. I like to make decisions on my own but it is rather a lot. Moving house and rebuilding added to that, and was in fact like a fourth job. During fourteen days of vacation I discovered how vulnerable I was in that moment, how tired. My facade of being efficient, alert, focused on doing and making decisions, being there for others, disappeared. I broke down.

'And then something wonderful happened: I got into deep contact with nature. All of a sudden it was there, just like that; like a huge gift. I realised I had worked towards this all these years, longed and yearned for it. The crazy thing is that somehow I had always known that an open communication with everything around me had to be possible. As a child in my little hiding place I had been close to the natural life around me. But later on so much happened that I hid my heart more and more, cut myself off from nature. So I would like to work through some old pain with you.' With a big sigh I look at Martha expectantly.

Yes, it started there. In Switzerland something in me had broken open, something I had longed for all my life. To be closer to the essence of life. Via various roads and crossroads on my life path I had now ended up here. With, as a result, the choice — or was it still a choice at this stage? — to open myself to a wholly different life. For it was clear that my life was changing, with all the ensuing consequences. What that life was going to look like wasn't at all clear, for I had entered a territory that was unknown to me, without precedent.

And there I am in the middle of the night sitting opposite her. She looks at me and says: 'Incredible you have come to me right now.' She has become convinced that our communication with nature is of real importance, for without it the world will perish.

Her big worry: because of people's behaviour the earth will be destroyed by natural catastrophes, humanity will perish along with it on a mass scale. People have polluted, abused and failed to appreciate the earth to such an extent that the volcanoes are going to erupt again, the oceans flood the land, storms wreak the utmost havoc. This year even, a tidal wave will rise out of the ocean and destroy everything along the coast of San Francisco, earthquakes will follow . . . The earth is angry, she says. Only the odd individual here and there, those who are in real contact with nature, will survive. 'Like you and me.' Oh. I sit there and listen to all this.

It's a nice mouthful for my guilt feelings as a human being towards the earth, as a partner in the destruction! Martha says I am not part of it now that I talk with nature . . . This is really weird . . . This doesn't fit . . . It only increases my confusion. One thing I know for sure and I say irritably: 'The earth has no judgement and so cannot be angry with us.' And what I don't dare say aloud is that I don't like elitist thinking. We decided to go to bed and continue talking the next morning. She in her little house, further on in the woods, I where I am, alone. After breakfast and a solitary morning walk through a really desolate landscape I see Martha arriving in her jeep. Did I find everything, and has the stove been lit? Indeed this morning I was woken up by a very resolute noise made by sure hands that performed a routine act. But I didn't know what they were doing. It was warm though when I came downstairs into the pleasant kitchen.

Towards lunchtime we settle down on a bench in one of the small, dark rooms to begin what I came for. She asks me to talk, simply to start with what comes up in me. But very soon she takes over from me and it appears that she wants to get her story out. She is furious that she doesn't have direct contact with nature and the invisibly present energies. 'Everybody has contact with these "beings" and I haven't!' I think she is joking but she is really angry. For years now with Elsie she has been making contact with the unseen energies via that little table or she asks for answers to her questions using a medium. But communicating directly she has not been able to do. 'I hear nothing, nothing!' The story about the nature catastrophes she had heard from a medium with whom she worked a lot.

'What do you hear when you walk around here? Is there something I need to know?' Impatiently she drags me off, up into the jeep and to her house. She wants me to listen to what her favourite tree has to say. The oak next to which she has built her house and which has become sick on one side. When I have to hear something or when somebody has high expectations, I get anxious. It conflicts with the tranquillity and the deep connection of communication. I wonder whether I really want this? Is she using me? Yes, of course she is. But it feels petty to refuse her. Like: I can hear this and you can't. As if suddenly a power factor comes into play. But proving I can do it gives me the creeps, it simply isn't about that. With some hesitation I say hello to the old oak who is standing there next to her house reaching for the sky with his rough, gnarly, bare branches. I ask why he is dying on one side, for it is obvious that he is. I hear the answer as a voice that resonates in me. The voice says: 'I need Martha to say that I don't have to suffer because there is suffering all around me.' At first it seems so insignificant because of the simple truth of it. And because all this is still very new for me, I doubt whether I have heard it correctly.

Martha's reaction is in fact spontaneous: 'No, of course not! Dear tree, of course not', she says aloud to the tree. To myself I think: you see, I can't listen properly with all that commotion from her. But as the day proceeds it dawns on me more clearly that I have heard very well. Doesn't Martha suffer unconsciously with the suffering of others? Doesn't she go along with it and her surroundings with her? A heavy pressure wraps itself around my stomach area and my head. I get terribly tight in the chest.

It is the last day of the year.

We decide to say goodbye to the old year at the European time. She doesn't like champagne, I have the excuse of jet lag, so why don't I just go to bed?

In reality I am feeling sick from the heavy pressure on my stomach. I feel utterly lonely. And angry. And disappointed. That Martha might need more attention at this time than she can give. I no longer feel at all like processing my wretched bits with her and I feel it is not sensible either; but I did cross the whole ocean for it. I become more and more confused. Why then did I come here? This week, with this woman? It had seemed such a good idea and safe. The opposite is true. I have lured myself into a trap.

It is cold upstairs and the water in the shower stinks of sulphur, or is it sewage? I can never tell those two apart.

To bed? Reading? Oh, it's so cold here!

The telephone. Thank God there's a phone, I'm sure I have seen one somewhere there in that other ice-cold upstairs room. Even in this abandoned place there is the possibility of communication. Making contact with something that belongs to me. Something warm and familiar. Even though I am totally alone in this godforsaken, ramshackle wooden house, I still feel guilty about wanting to talk with the outside world. What is it that gives me the feeling that I am doing something bad? Who is watching me? Come on. I can phone a friend to say happy new year, can't I? That's what telephones are for after all. This looks like the end of the world but the people I love are also somewhere. People? There is only one I want to hear now in this moment, hear very close by. With fingers shaking from the cold, I dial the long number. 'Hallo, it's me,' I hear on the other end. Aah . . . that sounds so nice, just what I need. 'Happy new year,' and there comes all my misery pouring out. 'It's cold here. I'm sitting in a small wooden house in some godforsaken dump. What? I'm with Martha. Yes, all alone. For a week.' A deep listening silence on the other end. 'She lives some way away in the woods. I wanted to tell her how I was doing.' 'Why her?' 'Well I think, or anyway I thought,' I add softly, 'that she is the ideal person with whom I can work through that old stuff. I want to get rid of it. She . . .' 'Who?' 'Martha herself has got all kinds of stuff. She is enormously worried about the earth. Foresees catastrophes. She told me about her absolute conviction that the earth would fall apart from neglect, abuse . . .' and so I tell the whole story, up to and including the idea that we would be caught up in the destruction. Except for a few like in Noah's Ark.

'She can't say that. She's talking about a dying earth. She is more preoccupied with death than with life. But you, do you want that? Be careful, Irene, you are getting caught in a web. She is of course always involved with sick people whom she is helping to die, all that negative energy of fear and disease stays with her if she doesn't let it wash away. It looks like she actually holds on to it with her thought-forms. As you are so totally on your own, you could get trapped in it. She is a bridge too far.'

All at once I see it very clearly and understand what is happening. Martha obviously once made the choice not to enjoy life any more, not to love life any longer. In her mind she was convinced that one person doesn't have to suffer because another is having a difficult time. Nothing was more true! You help nobody by abusing yourself because a group of people are being oppressed. By getting sick with the sick, miserable with the grief of another. Sitting by their side, listening, being there, that's what Martha was schooled in. Tirelessly she could listen and be there. Detached, especially because you are detached from the pain of the other, thus you help a person in need. That was and is useful. But in the long run, because of the amount of misery in this world, and knowledge of the soul world after death, she was more preoccupied with there than the here-and-now. Life itself. She didn't suffer with the suffering but had stepped out of life. After life was limitless love. There lived the guides with whom she talked via her mediums, there was a world for which she burned with desire. This earth she actually only saw as a torment. She couldn't live in it. Hence the stories about the end of the world, destruction, the angry earth. The oak went along with her, had embodied her choices, as it were, and directed his energies towards the afterlife with the result that he was dying here. Wasn't this precisely the same choice I was facing? Wasn't this exactly why I had come here?

I was caught in the trap of my own choice. Irrevocably.

What else do I want?

How can I go on?

What is it about for me?

What do I want to aim for with all that I now know?

Is it an either/or choice? Life here or what comes after it?

He is right, it is dangerous for me in such a fundamental moment of decision to be isolated here. His voice goes on talking: 'The earth is patient. The earth is love and we are not falling to pieces. Imagine, she just sweeps aside people's own free will. What we can break we can make. That's exactly it. It's all about choices. The earth will never fall to pieces. If it would, I would know,' his voice laughs, 'you too. Who would remain, she and who else? I wouldn't want to be one of them for sure!' Silence.

'How long did you want to stay there?' 'A week . . .' 'That's a long time.' 'Yes . . .' 'Take a good look at it!' Bye, bye dear indestructibly positive friend. Bye there, far away but now warm inside me. Thank you for your images, your support and clarity, your freedom and being part of me. But there it is, I am here for a week, I can't just leave, can I?

Well, maybe I'm here to get rid of my own negativity in the

midst of all the negativity present in this place. Like seeks like. Then I can leave it here. That's what I wanted, wasn't it? And besides, I can't leave. I can't do that. She has reserved time for me, who knows what she cancelled . . . I decide to remain. In this case not a free choice but one resulting from standards of politeness. A choice, after all.

4. Waking Dream

In the autumn night
When there's no wind blowin'
I could hear the stars falling in the dark
When you find what's worth keeping
With a breath of kindness
Blow the rest away.

Robby Robertson, *The Red Road Ensemble*

There is another person I want to call to wish a happy new year. Once more I dial a number, not so long this time. She is there as well. The moment I hear her voice asking how I'm doing, my emotions come rushing out. 'I'm not doing well. I don't know whether I can handle the negativity around me on my own. I'm here for a week still. I'm actually damned scared. Maybe I need to be here to give my own negativity a chance to emerge. Like seeks like . . .', and again I tell all the details of my visit to Martha . . . 'That's questionable. It could also be that it really isn't good for you there any more. You know how you can work through things on your own. You have the strength for it too. You can only do that in your own time, in your own space. If you don't want to stay, then leave. You've done that before. I even thought you were very good at it,' her soft clear voice says with a smile.

'Perhaps you have learned what you wanted to learn there.' I feel how her voice and words touch me once more, give me exactly the little push I need to come back into my knowing, out of the politeness choice. Out of the choice that is turned away from myself. Back to my own inner voice. 'You're right. I can leave. I can always leave. I'll find a way to get to the air-port, get tickets and so on. Yes, of course I can leave. Tomor-row morning I am going.' 'If you don't feel like being alone at home you can come here. I have to work but you know I always have time for you. What I can offer you here is the ocean, endless water, the sound of waves, space. You're wel-come.' 'I'm going home, thank you. You are very, very sweet. I'd like to call you to tell you how I organise my return jour-ney.' And then more quietly: 'Bye, bye, bye . . . and a happy new year.' Click, once more that warmth of contact, of hear-ing each other. Amazing to have reached these two people on this evening. Two creative realists. One has the all-encom-passing overview and keeps me centred in that, the other lis-tens and lays the cards on the table, both touch my inner cur-rent of strength.

Tomorrow I'm going to phone all the numbers I can think of to get away from here. I will find a way. No politeness. This is about something more important than that. My decision is made and already I feel like another person. I can breathe again. And darned if I can't see my own breath, it's that cold. With my socks on I climb into bed.

It is ice-cold and I am lying in a strange bed
in a foreign country
in between worlds and times
between old and new
between day and night
between waking and sleeping
all alone
only two amazingly big lumbering St Bernard dogs are keep-ing watch outside.
Tired I close my eyes, sleep I want, sleep at last.

But in the dark of the night I see something big and dark hanging above me; it slowly takes the shape of a huge and deadly tarantula. The hairy legs are reaching for my neck, closer and closer.

In my thoughts I try to put a shield between myself and the giant spider. But it makes the spider even fiercer. I don't feel up to this! Tomorrow I'm leaving, I don't care about this stuff. I get really angry and say aloud that I don't want this! I feel for the light switch that has to be somewhere near the bed, I find it and switch on the night light. Ah, there is nothing, of course there is nothing. Only rotten images in this rotten place! Damn it! I get up and go and have a pee.

Now I feel how cold the freezing night is and how chilled I am through and through. I get a few more blankets, hoping that will make the bed a bit more comfortable. I want to sleep. I get back under the blankets and, determined simply to go to sleep now, switch off the light.

To my tired consternation the spider is still there waiting for me . . . And now images of crawling snakes and dead skulls are appearing as well. One after the other is filing by and looking at me. It's very clear there is no getting away from this if I don't look at it and go through it. All the evil, the rottenness, human diseases are filing past me like pictures. Hands try to grab me . . . Sticky slimy things search for my body. I shrink up into a little ball of misery, as small as possible. and all over I feel the cold penetrating my bones. Around me I hear how it cracks, there in the left corner, behind the wooden walls; above me on the thin roof something is clearly slithering. And now the dogs in the yard start barking loudly as if at a poacher or a thief or something more frightening . . . Martha said I didn't have to fear anything unless the dogs barked . . .

In a flash I understand that I let all this into my life very early on and so it is now a part of myself, what is crawling there around me. If I don't accept it I will be caught, for sure. I start shedding my own misery as a snake does its skin. Bit by bit. Memories like crazily clear slides come filing by, with portraits of the people connected with them. People I'm angry with, moments of furious jealousy, situations of unprocessed fear and fury, outrage, narrow-mindedness . . .

Amidst these images the faces of the friends I was in

contact with just now are going past as a kind of comforter. Following them the image of a thin man, one thin shoulder pulled up, dressed in dirty white, in a wheelchair with high wheels which he clutches with his bony hands and pushes forward with strength. He is a lawyer. He accuses the world, the pollution, the destruction. I feel how my body relaxes every time I recognise something, every time I greet my own fears and insights into what I have done because of those fears. My reactions to it. There is an incredible clarity about it: why I acted as I did. A wave of mildness flows my way, judgement gives way to gentleness. Slowly, very slowly and carefully, I am able to stretch first one leg then the other, relax my back, my shoulders, my arms. The fear is gone. The tarantula too. And the snakes, the skulls, the fingers, the things. I have indeed shed a skin. Straight through the shadow side of the snake, the deadly poison, I have gone. What is on the other side?

I feel the life force flowing through me, the sap of life like a clear mountain stream is beginning to take the place of the processed dirt. It is taking up more and more space. I greet this counterforce with my whole being, the tingling of life, of movement, of growth. As strong as at first the images outside and around me were, the power of the joy of life is presently coming from within and through me. My strength, my joy! I have come through this wholly under my own power!

The trip to Martha's has not been for nothing. I had walked into the arms of death and had therefore sought the dying companion in order to encounter, dramatically and clearly, my own life force. With my back against the wall I had to make a choice. Naturally I could only do this alone. What a wonderful path of growth I have travelled these last two years: the encounter with nature, the doubt and the depression regarding my human duality. At first sunk deep into the darkness of myself, and then choosing the confrontation with duality, irresistibly, for life. The life in everything. My God, how strong I am.

Tonight something definitive has happened.

It is quiet. I sigh and relax even more.

Only the dogs are barking every now and again. I listen to

them attentively. What are they barking at? It is as if they are barking at their own echo in the immense space. Didn't I do that too? In my mind I tell the two big St Bernard dogs outside that it is over.

It is completely quiet now.

The frosty night has changed into a clear day.

I get up, pick up my things and, sparklingly aware of my positive strength, I walk into life. To meet the sun.

Tuesday 28 Jul.
—

I suggest we convene in Victoria Road
slightly after 2? o'clock for a 2.15 start.
Performance starts at 5.45.
Let me know if you're on chairs +
make area chez Pen Leith

16/7

© **MARTIN COOPER**
'Frank's Banjo'
Oil on Board 41 × 34 cm
Telephone 051-625 5711

5. Afterwards

*Know that the little droplet that you represent is being
accepted by the whole.*

David Carson

I am lying in an ancient, very ancient, spot. A beach on the
southeast coast of England. I am visiting a very sweet friend
with an Aga stove. Everything here is gentle. The sun won't
burn me, the wind won't blow anything to pieces, the sand of
the earth is of the finest soft yellow grain and the water is like
velvet.

Sea inlet with high and low tide. You can hear the tides by
their gentle murmuring. Inexorably to and fro, up and down,
a lot and a little, generous and withdrawn, reaching out and
come-and-get-me, wet and dry, covering and uncovering the
ugly bottom. Lying here among the four elements I feel part of
it. I feel that I am everything and nothing at the same time.
Material body and airy energy. Part of everything and yet an
individual with her own past, a unique history of joyful and
sorrowful experiences, inescapably up and down. This primordial spot brings up profound feelings in me and is full of
sand-fleas. Do the sand-fleas jump like that because they are
naked? The transparent little bodies, used to being unseen
beneath the earth, seem to be at odds with the light. They hop
around like blind, out-of-control lunatics. What would they look
like if they lived in the light for a while?

In her bed Elizabeth lies among soft cushions, a hundred
per cent linen. A delicate grey light shines through the big windows which are divided into small squares by narrow white-

painted leading.

It is her birthday.

She is alone.

Sadness in her eyes about that being alone. Friendship counts, then. Warmth. After hesitating slightly I crawl in next to her. Why don't we do this any more? Oh miserable puritanism! What is more natural than two bodies against each other to ease the pain. That helps a lot. A cup of tea in bed. Breakfast with just the most delicious things. Rose, named after your mother, beams deep red at you, with two buds bursting open.

The wind makes the poplar leaves murmur like the sea. What tale do you tell? Of full ripe summers. Of always being present, faithful, just being there, always. Until you are no longer there, or we.

'Then there is something else? What?'

'It doesn't matter. Something else anyway, different from now.'

'To whom are you telling this?'

'To whomever wants to hear it. That's the same as whomever can hear it. The animals hear a lot.'

'Do they care what they hear?'

'No.'

Only I, a human with my dualistic thinking capacity, think. Grind, grind, grind like a flat grinding stone, big and heavy. With bare feet on the grass. Toes are feeling deep in green and flowers. Liquid. What am I doing here? Friendship. Because I want to be here. It is healing, here I find pieces of myself. Here I can open my heart a little more again, let go of some of the fear of the consequences of feeling. Everything except total surrender that would fit the moment. House, land, rhythm, habits. Possessiveness. My way is best. Do you fit into my little boxes? I don't want to make too many concessions any more. I've had enough of them. I've been stretched and dried out by them to breaking point. I'm doing so well right now. But just the same, being alone is only fun when it's from choice.

Alone?

Doing what I feel like doing. Not having to do my best to be there for someone else at every moment. No bother, no criticism, having to explain, being careful. Being joyful when I feel joyful, as much as I want to be. Just like that . . . Especially no explanation.

Birthdays, what are they actually? Being there for others, dead tired and empty to bed after sitting in a circle eating cakes that are too sweet and drinking too many cups of tea and coffee? Birth-day. Birth! Hey, there you are. Glad you are here. Glad I can come today and celebrate your existence. That you were born. That you want to be on this earth. Receive! Learn to receive and don't do anything today. Are you happy to be here? Tell me, tell me. I love listening to you, feeling you trust me with it. Your stories about how you think and where you get your ideas from. Your history built up out of the rules of your parents and their parents, your country, your soil and the wind.

Sun, hallo! You are a radiant conversation partner. Hard and honest. That particularly and you too without that perpetual judgement, that distortion of what I really mean. No, I shall never be alone again. Never. And yes, I always need people around me. But the right ones. And not always, that's not possible any more. I will listen to you, sun. And to the others. The stone. The tree . . .

Child of the sun. Part of you, sun. Elizabeth is part of the water. Water child. You belong with it. You feel at home with it, familiar. In some way or other you know this element better than the others. Me, I was always scared of water. I don't really know it. Up until a certain moment somewhere in my thirties, I used to have a terrible dream about a tidal wave that came rolling in on the immense grey sea and that could reach me any time, wash over me. Under that force I would try again and again to get air but I would be smashed up relentlessly under the immensity of all that dark water. Against that superior power I knew myself to be totally powerless. Until that dream came where I was boating in a little white motorboat with my best friend and a couple of trusted girlfriends. The sun was shining in a steel blue sky. The water of the endless sea was clear green. In the distance we saw land with high, weathered, green-grey stone houses. Out of the distance the metres-high, merciless wave came towards us in our small boat, closer and closer. Like a huge green wall it rose above the surface of the water . . . There it hung, waiting like a cobra instead of catching us. Then suddenly the wave got smaller and smaller, until it dissolved completely in the water. We approached an island that was composed of a white, futuristic, long, low, immensely huge building. A new land. I got off, the friends went on.

That wave, that threat, never came back after that.

Yes, the sun is familiar to me. She returns my greeting with an extra little beam of brightness. For a short while a little bit warmer. And cherishes me down to my pores. Like a cat stretching itself, the sun nestles around me, against me. The wind helps too. We are made out of the elements, are part of them. Dust becomes matter and then dust again. Puff! Once more part of it all, invisible now, yet tangible. Before long, when I have gone puff, those who remain living on the earth will still be able to sense me, but as pure energy. Until I have gone somewhere else, further on. In between two lives, as if it were the interval in a theatre performance, we agreed to meet each other again when through freedom of spirit we had become conscious of what inner freedom is. We met up in England at the train station. Our ages and lives were different. We came from different cultures but had acquired the same insights.

The poplars whisper, the sun and the clouds play their game, the bumble-bees drink the nectar from deep within the flower.

In the middle of the night I wake up, sit up in my bed and sense what's the matter. I get an image of a big old-fashioned sailing ship, one of those lumbering things with a lot of sails. It's clear to me that this image represents my life. While I am watching it, seeing the bow cut through the water, the colours of water and bow in blues and greens, the heavy thing lurches slowly. Actually it's less than that, it prepares itself to tack. But it's enough of a sign for me to know that my life is changing course. I can hardly believe it. Could the difficult times really be over? . . .

For a long time I continue to watch this image, following it with my eyes. Realising, understanding, and then it slowly dawns on me that, if I see this so clearly, I have to believe it as well. And, more important still, that I can trust this image. I don't often have such clear visual images. The turning point came in America, after I had processed a lot of stuff . . . And if I trust that this is really true, then it *is* so. That's the way it works, isn't it? 'Hold the vision,' a very old acquaintance tells me. He explains that if you do not hold something in your thoughts and visualise it, it cannot materialise. 'Hold the vision and everything is possible.' Again after the same delay I feel the joy coming up. A new course! A new era! Downstream now. Past, further, different! A new part of my life! No longer heavy. Presently in my full consciousness and feeling I lie down again, ready to sleep. But first I ask the eagle who lives in this valley to give me a sign of confirmation of what I have seen, to help me really believe in it, by showing itself in the morning. Non-believer that I am.

Over a rather late breakfast outside in the morning sun we are sitting talking about the most banal things, a friend and I. It irritates me slightly that the night was so meaningful and I can't really share it with her. That the conversation is so trivial. While talking she points at the sky: 'Look!' And there is the golden eagle flying majestically in big circles. My mouth falls open, my heart misses a beat. There he is. Communication! He is flying his circles closer and closer to us, directly over the house. There he goes round three times and swoops straight down towards the other side of the valley. Slowly and quietly, sure of his flight.

These are connections you can overlook or notice. Meaningful? Yes!

The eagle is equally regarded as the sun, messenger of the angels . . . The Chinese say that three signifies totality, perfection. Christians say: God is three in one.

Well, well!

That same summer miracles happen. It looks as if the road is rising with me. What seems scary beforehand turns out to be a delightful event. Where do miracles come from? Do they really fall out of heaven? It only looks like that because in such a moment you forget all you have done to make a miracle possible. Simply talking to a flower without thinking up your own answer doesn't come of itself. People you haven't talked to for a long time and who are getting closer to you again, neither. But the miraculous feeling remains a delight!

I am sitting on a soft green patch of grass in the high mountains. Flowers around and under me. Purple, dark red, sunny yellow, tender delicate white, gentians with their deepest sky-blue as balm for the soul. Alone I sit, amid the immensity of the old, wise, powerful and eternally alive mountains. A huge expanse above and around me. Endless surfaces in space surround me. Timeless and yet in the now. Here I am in this moment, probably a bit difficult to reach until all this has become part of me, then I am once more available for whoever wants to understand. Meanwhile I enjoy the sun and the view and I stretch my legs comfortably. Sun, caress my skin and give me light. Wind, touch me and play with me. Water, heal my wounds. Earth with your stones and your grit, your flowers, your worms and your butterflies, give me security. A place to lie down and to breathe in utmost contentment.

Confirmations are more meaningful to me than the evidence science requires. My own evidence I get in loving abundance.

This year there are a great many flowers. They lean towards the last of the sunlight. Above me a wall of rock towers like a prehistoric reptile. This tranquillity and security of nature is transient. Everything can simply start moving and you can't insure yourself against that. Is this not eternity?

Back in the Netherlands the question keeps nagging me of how I can keep in touch with the natural world. What I had some success with out and up there is suddenly difficult again down here. The house and all that happens within it devours all my attention. Indoors the interpersonal communication is excellent. But I no longer go outdoors. On the one hand because of all I have to do, but equally because the garden is a fenced-in piece of nature. I am no longer called outside. The connection with the whole of nature is lacking and so I find it more difficult to make contact. As if all of a sudden I am living on an island formed by my house and the garden around it without the authenticity of nature. How do the trees and the water experience this?

I sense grief in the trees, for the boundary lines seem more important than they do. People take more notice of the fence and who sits behind it than they do of nature. You can't change human nature with all its curiosity, jealousy and envy. But if, as well, people were to talk with trees and listen to water, were to smell and marvel, were to connect in all these ways with their fellow inhabitants of the earth, this would give space to the trees, the space of being. And humans would acquire an extra dimension.

The old copper beech says I am starting to get it and I sense something like a sigh.

A big double-decker dragonfly swishes past me, comes back time and again and then flies in square circles around me. A pale-grey little body, four large transparent wings divided into minuscule parts like scores of little windows. Every now and then it hovers in the air and hums at me with its big eyes. What are you trying to tell me? I make myself very quiet inside and try to sense what it is communicating. I notice particularly how much the little animal is in its centre and how from that centre it can go in all directions.

For the native North American the essence of the dragonfly stands for breaking through illusions. Therefore to them it is a messenger of change. There is a beautiful legend that tells how the dragonfly was once a dragon and very wise.* He flew through the night and broke up the light with his fiery breath. Through the breath of the dragon the art of magic and the illusion of metamorphosis came to life. The dragon got trapped in his self-delusion; he accepted a challenge to prove the power of his own magic and turned into a dragonfly, thereby losing his power.

When the dragonfly comes near you, according to them, you have to look at what needs to change in your life. They attribute healing powers to animals and all living things and call this their 'medicine'. I can begin to comprehend this, what with all my experiences. With all this wisdom in the back of my mind I end up with the thought of being connected with each other spiritually. The dragonfly is asking me to do this with the essence of all that lives and grows. Then I hear very clearly: 'Believe in yourself, your own centre.' Each time I hear such a voice resonate inside myself with some kind of wise message, I am amazed all over again and thankful for the new communication. Anyway these days I feel myself at the centre of a house full of growing children and friends of the children. A lively situation with so much significance. A group of wise people together for whom I am a grateful and implicit centre. With them I communicate from my centre, with nature too but they are two different worlds for sure. One belonging indoors and the other outdoors. If I understand the dragonfly well, I may drop that separation and let the inside and the outside always be there. I am going to practise this, for I feel that in this way I approach a central point which could allow me to ease the painful transition from outdoor life to 'everyday

---

* See Jamie Sams/David Carson, *Medicine Cards, The Discovery of Power Through the Ways of the Animals*, Bear & Co

life'. Firstly, in some way keeping life inside the house open to nature. I imagine that the energies from outside can simply flow straight through the house, that the walls of the house don't have to be barriers to it. Just as the boundaries of the garden are there only for people and not for the plant and animal worlds. Later I practise having conversations with people without cutting myself off from the world out there and the elements.

Thank you dragonfly.

The gardener had almost taken away the little peach tree that grows against the wall of our house. It looks as if it wanted to show us how glad it is to be alive, for this year it stood bowed with fruit, a bucketful of it.

A further step is to allow the elements into your body. Slowly letting the energy of the sun penetrate the surface of your skin, into your organs, into all the cells of your body and all your veins, up to and including your bones. Similarly with water, air and earth. Then feeling what it all does to you. What colours come with it, what feelings. What it does with my body: does it relax, does it get warm or cold, light or heavy, does it make me glad or is there some pain that needs to come up? . . . First I start with one organ or one chakra. I choose the eyes, for they are full of old turbidity.

OK, here goes: I invite the sunbeams to penetrate my closed eyes. I let the orange rays bathe the tensed-up little muscles. The craziest thoughts thwart and sabotage the process: the sun blind still needs to be ordered(!), the heating is on too high, wasn't the plumber going to come round? How delightful that orange light is. I wonder how Marieke is doing? . . .

Are these thoughts in my retina and do they come out because of the sun-bath, or do my thoughts rove around at random? Both, I think. It's difficult to concentrate fully, being only and totally in the here and now. Deeper and deeper I let in the patient sun. A deep relaxation ensues. Some water is necessary to make it all flow a bit, make it more playful. I imagine water playing through my eyes and it is delightful. Your imagination, your imaginative power, is the instrument of your soul. How much we can give each other! At least, the sun is giving to me. What do I give? Trust, love, gratitude, I offer myself openly. And what happens if I equally let in the energy of the copper beech? It takes practice to be able to focus all your attention on just one tree, on the sun alone, on that one dragon-fly exclusively. Not to think of anything else, to empty yourself and be alert at the same time. Open to some kind of message, in whatever unexpected form, just from what you are focusing on.

By concentrating all your attention, that tree or whatever it is you are focused on, starts to radiate much more strongly. The energy is stepped up. When you simply hold a stone in your hand, the effect is completely different from when you give that same stone all your attention. It is exactly the same with people: when you get real attention you start radiating, you are more yourself.

It said in the newspaper that a butterfly sees more colours than we humans do. They seem to see ultraviolet rays as well. 'We' are able to see and feel a lot more than we think, it is a question of cleansing our 'potential for clarity'; then, just like the butterfly, we will see the colours around things. The non-urban cultures are certainly a lot more capable of this, there is much to be learned from them too.

The fear of living with my negativity is over. The undermining confrontation with reality. My passionate fight against the evil in the world, the injustice, was actually a fight against my own injustice, my quick and often ruthless judgement. My own neg-ativity, jealousy, destructiveness, I didn't notice for a long time. The hate, misery, the pain of the world, I fought against it like a Joan of Arc or a medieval knight. The battle against EVIL. It shouldn't exist and because it did it had to be fought! Now I know that creativity and destruction are indissolubly connect-ed with each other because they are each other's counterparts. As if they are sitting back to back in the middle of one circle. They are each other's backs. We humans can all make and break, create and kill. The Saddam Husseins of the world are ideal for distracting our attention from our own destructive side. It is nice to think: he is bad and you and I are not. Almost always, when you point a finger, when you fiercely condemn something in another, it is about a characteristic you don't accept in yourself, with which you don't want to be confronted. That is a given nowadays.

I notice that, by accepting my own destructive side, I can use this force in a positive sense. The amount of energy it took simply to deny my rage . . .

For remarkably enough you can transform the enormous power of the urge to destroy into positively directed creativity, *if* you accept it. It is incredible and staggering that you shut away such a large part of yourself because it makes you sick and you disapprove of it and as such don't use it in another way.

Isn't it true that human creative potential through conscious choice would add something to the cosmos which the creative level of plants and animals does not have because they do not know duality? Isn't it true that the primordial element, the primordial light, needs nourishment via this duality consciousness? To me, one level does not seem superior to the other, only different with different purposes. Nature exists with endless patience. Older and wiser than we humans. People are more ephemeral beings. Newcomers on earth. Inundation, fire, earthquakes, eruptions are not 'bad'! Yet it is destruction. But nature does not do all this out of malice. There is no judgement in it. We humans call nature ruthless, yet this is a human concept. When *we* destroy something, we do it from a subconscious or conscious choice. There is judgement in it and a matching emotion (*furiously* he hits her for he *thinks* she is a stupid old tart). A tree simply cannot think in such a way! An erupting volcano is not an outburst of rage from the depths of the earth because of what we humans are doing to that earth. If this were the case, the power in the earth would long since have wiped us out. People perish in an earthquake. We find this terrible. Yet that is something totally different. It is human

thinking and feeling. All other life has a very different consciousness. A non-dualistic consciousness that is never cut off
from the primordial source and as such cannot react in terms
of 'bad' or 'good'. Only we humans do good and evil from a
conscious level. And therein, in my view, lies the essence of
our being human. In our consciousness there is this freedom
of choice. Good and bad are a constant challenge and give
unlimited possibilities for choice. When as a human being you
accept your own duality, your destructive and your creative
power, then this strengthens the unity of the contradiction in
you and thus you grow. You strengthen the primordial principle, the light in you. Or, when the duality disappears (be it
only for a moment) because you accept it, in that moment you
are an integrated part of the primordial source, which in its turn
is strengthened by it.

It becomes very clear to me that we human beings, with
our consciousness that is different from that of the other life-
forms on this planet, are part of each other within a human
group consciousness and equally part of 'the rest'. I think that
every 'species' (trees, flowers, rocks, animals, etcetera) has a
group consciousness. Each is unique of its kind. And that we
are a sub-part of a whole that is ever in movement. Pulsating,
vibrating, rhythmic. Changing, growing. Everything together
forms one whole with a distinct purpose, united in one all-
encompassing goal. This purpose is none other than *being*
who we are.

The more we are ourselves and the closer to our inner light,
the closer we are to our connection with the light in all life.

Martha wants more contact with nature so that the earth
does not perish. I see it differently: for me it is all about love.
The contact with the essences of life around us, 'nature', brings
us humans into contact with the essence of everything: love.
Unconditional, limitless love where good and bad don't come
into it, for it is not dualistic. It is there and we do not see it. But
when we see and experience it, our life changes, we make
completely different choices and we deal in a new way with
our living environment. It brings us into contact with the emo-

tional life of the world outside the walls of our home and consequently into contact with our own emotions. When some of your feelings are locked up, in the end you live only partially. It brings us into contact with the whole of ourselves, with the source of light in ourselves.

I assume that all that lives here on earth always lives, *somewhere*. That what dies here exists somewhere else. Nothing is ever 'gone'. Everything is always 'somewhere', only in a different form from on earth.

So the person who no longer lives here on earth will be somewhere else in another form. I picture that form as a movement, a vibration that matches the thought-forms and the essence of that person. Here on earth we are a solidified form of that vibration because we have incarnated in a body, we became part of the material earth. Just as the trees or a flower did. Our material form tells us a lot about how and who we are, just as a tree through its form shows how and who it is.

Contact with nature is important to me, not for fear that the earth will explode, nor for fear of dying. In my opinion everything continues to exist anyway and, who knows, it might even be more fun. Contact with nature is important to me because, if we continue treating the earth and each other and ourselves with lack of respect and feeling, we use only a part of ourselves. The 'non-communicating' part. Nature teaches us what it is to live in oneness. And as we become more familiar with this we can focus more on the part in us which is connected with all of life. This makes life more enjoyable not only for ourselves but equally for all that is alive around us. In this way I have experienced how dolphins show us what it is to live carefree in the face of knowledge of the world's sorrow. Through the simple fact that they live in the now, it becomes a lot easier.

Everybody can contribute to the development of the light in all these little cells. We can infuse more life into it. And this is a powerful contribution precisely because we do it of our own choice. Every thought, every deed has an effect on the whole right up to the furthest little out-of-the-way corner of the cosmos. Everything that lives has significance within the whole.

Does that make all this misery necessary? I think so. It is less important what we do than how we do it. The intention. The underlying emotion behind the actions. The consequences of our choices have repercussions on the whole of life. I think that growth is part of that limitless love. That love can grow too, 'learn' as it were. And we are part of that process.

My little Inside-voice says that because I have always worked very hard I haven't taken time to observe the spider gliding just in front of my eyes, little legs pulled up, right now when I am trying to free my eyes of the tension left over from my old way of seeing! Spiders continually make new webs, gossamer structures appear effortlessly out of their little bellies, their centre. And wham, there goes something straight through it and the whole creation is destroyed. But no panic: quietly, delightfully ignorant of any urge to prove itself or of any blame, it makes a new construction.

Looking at the little web affects me differently from looking at the small insect caught in its own web. To consider the little spider a prisoner right now is a choice. And so the whole day through I make choices that determine my life and which in their turn were determined by choices made earlier on in my life. Which then draw events and people that have something to do with those choices. A victim-conscious person or a gossamer-structure-oriented person: that leads to another kind of encounter. As time goes on I understand better and better how you draw to yourself what you send out, how much it is entirely up to you what your life looks like.

A cynical little voice says that this is a rather superficial way of thinking: 'And what about the people in Bosnia?' From our human perspective it sounds harsh but from the point of view that everything exists for ever and that we are here to learn lessons in all kind of situations, you may indeed say that it is part of it. Thus the people over there are learning something that is important for them, exactly as others are elsewhere. One situation is not worse or better than another, it is a circumstance you choose in which to learn what you need for your growth within the coherent whole of your learning process throughout your lives. Your learning process is, I think, indissolubly connected with that of others and with the learning process of the greater whole. The totality of growth.

And why do I see so many butterflies fluttering around me? That one over there looks rather like a piece of birch bark, only more yellow. Butterflies . . . transformation . . . Am I not in the process of changing my way of looking?

With a full diary it is difficult to notice these subtleties, this timelessness, let alone experience it. I am happy with the new balance I have built into my life by letting these moments of silence be a part of my worldly life of work and all the rest.

All these experiences are so refreshing, as if I were meeting new friends who tell me wonderful things. I ask the big copper beech to surround me with its energy for I am feeling a bit vulnerable during my transformation. A vibration is clearly visible and it looks as if the tree in all its magnificent grandeur is coming towards me. Nothing amazes me any more, for by now I am used to things happening which can only be unexpected, in fact, when I don't start from my human frame of reference. Naturally that copper beech doesn't wrap its branches supportively around me like a person would, but it moves its energy towards me and now I feel how the energy closes in a circle around me, warm and safe. Thank you, tree. In the process it shows me how far its branches spread out from its gigantic, playfully twisted trunk. Its centre. 'Any human can be just as vast, it bothers nobody when you are shining and vast like this.' Yes, I needed to hear this. What a delightful way to interact with each other!

The ever-present cynical little voice niggles inside me that this new reality of coming together will never be accepted in this cynical world. You may shrug your shoulders and say that it's too vague, too elusive, too strange . . . At best it is hard to believe. You can make up anything! For one or other reason people have to 'believe' things that come under the category of invisible. Belief is more or less the opposite of proof. It's sad, isn't it, this overbearing necessity of having to prove everything before it may be considered true. Tangible is true. Tangible and provable belong to the real world. The Bible itself said something about that doubting Thomas who had to touch things before he believed them. Didn't Jesus walk on the water because he had trust?

I am getting more involved with experiencing, playing with possibilities, making discoveries and enjoying myself while being amazed. Trust. Meanwhile I have received enough 'proof' . . . Enough to put two realities next to each other. The invisible one and the visible one. The fun part of it is that the more I get acquainted with the metaphysical, the more beautiful I find the visible and the tangible.

At first everything looked like a two-dimensional picture, but now I know that everything visible and tangible feels, vibrates and is connected with everything else and with the cosmos. The three-dimensional picture has become a multi-dimensional reality.

When you experience pleasure in this way, you feed the cosmos with pleasure-energy. If you enjoy life you are strong when disaster strikes. It is difficult to remain detached from somebody else's sorrow (Martha and her tree!). It is difficult to take pleasure in the peace of your home with your eyes filled with images of war. It is difficult to enjoy life while others are in hopeless situations. I try to enjoy life and I'm quite successful. But what about the newspaper?

May I withdraw? Is positive energy as strong in the universe as pity, suffering, sorrow? 'Sacred non-attachment,' said the old clairvoyant from the Hague. 'You can't take the misery of the world on your shoulders. For one thing it is very arrogant but also you cannot take on the responsibility of others. You would often like to do so but it is literally impossible.' How do you contribute positively to this world and the cosmos? . . . Flying doctors? Protest marches in your own country to demonstrate your solidarity against the violation of human rights elsewhere? Fighting for the good, against what to you seems bad? Writing articles about what is right? Being against? Being for? Working yourself to death to help people who are economically worse off? Working hard to help keep the economy going? Proposing political solutions to create a society that, to you, seems better? Or can it also be done by being joyous about all that is good, beautiful, tender? Joy gives tremendous nourishment to similar energy. Could there be a situation when precisely this would be the greatest contribution you could make? Everything is needed, nothing is wrong. It is just about what you want to fill your life with, what is important to you. It is not so much about what you do as about how you do it, and from what emotional context.

Our Calvinist way of thinking actually makes learning to enjoy ourselves very difficult. But who in fact am I helping when I grieve while there is so much around and in me to be enjoyed?

It is damned difficult to enjoy yourself! Just as the tree at Martha's needed to hear that you may enjoy yourself while others are having a difficult time, I need to hear it time and again. 'You may have a good time despite all the misery in the world.' Isn't this exactly what it is all about?

I consider myself stupid for not being able to enjoy myself and at the same time not contributing anything useful in this moment to help alleviate the misery. Help! Feelings of guilt block the way.

The voice of the friend opposite me in the Chinese restaurant is saying: 'How can anybody sense and locate the essence of things and simultaneously occupy themselves with making the world a better or worse place? You think you are doing nothing, apparently you aren't. To grasp the essence of why things like war happen in the world, you need silence. Silence to connect yourself with the essences. Your contribution in this moment is to understand why things happen. You don't take part in the war. You watch it and you worry . . . Watch! and let it be! War is total lack of communication with everything! By seeing that, you do "something".' Once more that 'sacred non-attachment'. A deep sigh; I am getting it.

Silence is for me a precondition for listening. And silence I only get through a certain tranquillity inside myself. That tranquillity I reach only through releasing the fighting, the struggle, the fear, the helping, the 'musts'. Then I take time to enjoy life, to live in and through the moment, the now. That is actually a contradiction in terms, for it is precisely the element of time that drops away when I am enjoying myself. Time is an illusion invented by people, say the wise.

When you enjoy life you radiate joy-energy into the cosmos and contribute to an equilibrium in the world. It is easier for me to tell this to someone else than to do it myself. I don't feel like helping any more. Working together with people in an open way in which no party has to be scared of knowing or having less, or of not being able to do something. For that I feel very much indeed. Working together, in the knowledge that you are always learning from one another and are sitting opposite each other precisely because of that. Exactly as I am doing now with nature. Every human, every plant, stone, water, animal has something to teach others from their own being. It requires an open attitude and a relaxation of the wall of fear built up by various wounds. It is all there and we don't see it. Just imagine if we humans were to lose our fear of being different from our normal selves and from each other . . . we would enjoy ourselves!

'Without nature we wouldn't exist. We need nature in order to live. Nature doesn't need us.' That is what a tree surgeon said and I fully agree with him. The misunderstanding that humans are the masters of nature, that nature needs the human race, has had tragic consequences. I wanted to write, 'What a pity,' but that is too cynical.

We treat nature like colonisers in a way . . . In the above-mentioned book about the powers of animals, it is stated clearly that if the human population increases further, 'we all have to get more closely acquainted with our environment'.* The author naturally means nature. In our culture our immediate surroundings are often asphalt and concrete, noise and pollution. At best it is a polluted nature, trees that are dying, water that harbours hardly any life, pastures that have turned sour, soil that has been trampled by many people. We can embrace the old Native American wisdom which stems from a worldview in which humans and nature are connected and live side by side. They are now asking for our cooperation! Hopefully their call will help too.

Not that we should go back to past times. Too much has happened for us to be able to imitate the old way of life. It is not about a romantic Rousseau-esque idea of 'back to nature'. We can no longer afford to be romantic, it is too late for that. In my view it is about finding a new way that matches our present reality and whereby we can indeed learn a lot from the old wisdom. Particularly from the way of life, respect and knowledge of all that lives with us.

The fact remains that people only learn when they experience something, live something, themselves. If I hadn't moved away from the busy life, oriented towards doing and external reality, to the inside, my inside, then I would, for instance, never have come across the booklet of the animal medicine cards and all the books published by Sun Bear. Or works by people like Rupert Sheldrake, Bede Griffiths, Michael Roads, Machaelle Small Wright, Joan Ocean, Jeffrey Goelitz, Gary Zukav . . .

It's a slow process, at least for people like me. Maybe this is indeed the challenge for humanity. Just a bird's eye view: At first we knew the equilibrium of the elements and lived by that. Then we lost that equilibrium and poisoned the world and nature with it. Now it is time to get back to the love that is in everything, to rediscover the harmony, the colour gradations, the rhythms, the energies, together with our own, and to live together.

---

*See Jamie Sams/David Carson, *The Medicine Cards, The Discovery of Power Through the Ways of the Animals,* Bear and Co.

Or do we, as individuals, experience these cycles together with the world? In my life it certainly looks that way.

Isn't it true that we don't appreciate what is a matter of fact? If a separation between 'good' and 'bad' had never taken place, we would indeed never have known that good was good. If night didn't follow day we wouldn't know what light is. Without noise you don't know what silence is, without disharmony what harmony is. After a masterpiece of disharmony created by human beings, it is hopefully time now to rediscover nature and make it into a talking partner, a teacher, a friend. And this can only happen individual by individual.

To put it in a pessimistic way: when we, here, make such a mess of things, not only do we and all of life on earth perish but we also send out a destructive power into the cosmos. Each and every person can decide not to be part of this. And the more people who do so, the more effectively it works. Together we create a positive power which concentrates itself as an energy field.

Put in a positive way: each one of us has the power to contribute, every moment of the day and night, to the creative transformation of the whole that we call life. The worst kind of pollution is that of our thoughts. So you can think for instance: it is as it is, we can't change it; or you can think: of course it can be different. We can replace negative thoughts by positive ones and this automatically gives different results. We can exchange our sorrowful image of a polluted earth for an image of a clean, healthy earth which is once again in balance because everything lives together. It would work miracles. We only have to look around us, open ourselves up, listen and dare not to know and shift our judgement a bit. In short: aim our thoughts at respect for all that lives. Would we then get to see a world in which Mankind is known as Kindman on the planet of Kindness?

It would indeed be history turned upside down if Westerners were to bring back harmony and be the leaders in this. New creation comes into being via chaos. Isn't that so? If human beings can create that total chaos, they are equally able to have something new be born from it. Men and women from all cultures, each in their own way. Here as well the differences in approach are fascinating and necessary. I hardly dare say it, but I do see changes coming.

Immediately I come up against an absolute asshole! Do I take it to heart or is something else the matter? Is it possible that there are people with whom you can't get on?

What is which element in the garden telling me? Quietly, quiet inside, listening.

A young hawthorn tells me I must forgive him.

'Ugh, that sounds so virtuous,' I say.

'You must let him be as he is and respect that.'

Good, that's more to my liking. A *Pyrus japonicus,* over a hundred years old, draws my attention and says: 'He is afraid and so are you. He can't be different in this moment and would like to be in your vicinity to see what it is you are doing.'

'What am I afraid of then?'

'Of getting hurt.'

'Yes, that's right and that's why I don't get involved in conversation with him.'

The *Pyrus japonicus* tells me that's all right, in its own words: 'Let him slide off you. Shake him loose.'

In the chestnut tree (almost bare, for it is autumn) the starlings play a little game of 'let's have fun falling down together'. Twittering joyfully they tumble straight down at breakneck speed, two by two. I'm not the fearful type but letting yourself fall like that . . . On this cool autumn morning I feel that this is precisely what I have done. I have changed my life completely. We can create our own life! We are fully responsible for all that happens to us. Disappointments about a man, a woman, about life's dreams which turned out so terribly different, I staged them myself. I have been furious about the misery, the injustice, the arrogance of leading figures in the world. The sad distribution of a bit of happiness.

I suppose we all have been everything, from king to prostitute, throughout different lives, and that we humans here on this planet are learning the lessons of duality. In the body of a man, a woman, in different cultures and times. Oppressor and oppressed. Ignorant or aware. With and without handicaps. Among man-made creations also belong wars, violence and oppression, like pus exuding from a wound. It is part of me for I am human too. Life is twisted and difficult, a struggle, a fight on many fronts. I know what I'm talking about. As part of that one human species, every decision you make, each thought you form, is part of that whole. Thus every single human being is important; so many people don't realise this. As I said before: if we form one body as a 'species', then every cell in that body can be a determining factor in the health of the whole.

You are really important! You matter!

When you decide not to be pitiful, no more a victim of circumstances, then you will no longer see the spider as a prisoner in her web of circumstances. You see rather how she has woven her own beautiful, unique web and now sits there waiting till some delicious little titbit comes her way.

Having limitless trust. Literally limitless in the trust that those things come to you which are good for you. Then they do come and your life becomes wonderful.

A lazy day in autumn. All alone in this delightful house where I live with my children. Lots of little jobs to do but nothing substantial. A feeling of emptiness gnaws at my insides. No fat sandwich will be able to fill this emptiness. During the time when I was married I sometimes felt the same.

It feels as if something is missing. A house full of children helps to keep this feeling at bay most of the time. But what about when, before long, they are not there any more? Is the hole going to become so big that I will fall into it? But last year I was already at the bottom. Not again, please. It wasn't very nice in there. Terribly dark and gloomy. Then I had absolute trust that I would get out of it again. I don't know whether I would have that again. A pitch-black butterfly in my room! What have you come to show me? 'Let go of your black thoughts!' Transform, yes. With a sigh I realise that I was again being sucked into a downwards vortex of thought.

Everything I have ever done brings me to where I am now. However simple it may sound, it's true. It's not unpleasant to feel that everything has had meaning. All those baffling, horrible, painful, hopeless, lonely, unsuccessful and yet glorious experiences were part of the path too. My path. Up to here and now. Years ago, in answer to my question of what for heaven's sake was life all about, someone said: 'The purpose of life is your path. You yourself are the path.'

Having released the structure of a job. The whole package of what comes after that as well. My son said: 'You are in search of the grail, you are now ready for it but you can't find it just like that. For when you search, you don't find. It's about an attitude to life. If you live in a certain way you find what you are looking for.' A wonderful person; indeed as individuals they all are. And what he says is very true and very wise. When you want something and search for it in a compulsive way you will not find it.

What is this attitude to life? How do I find it? Will it give substance to the rest of my life? Or is it nothing more than reinforcement of the 'delight level'? A kind of stabilising of enjoyment out of which I then live and experience further? One big question mark. Since I emptied myself totally, I sense in the quiet of the day what is waiting for me. What I am going to busy myself with. I no longer fit into the noisy life, nor am I able to live with a fully planned agenda. I end up in a whole new integration. One of my daughters has the rare gift of being able clearly to express her cosmic consciousness alongside her limited body consciousness, to be able to make comparisons between the two levels and to know where she stands between them. Presently she is taking her final examinations and needs all her attention to be able to concentrate on the subjects she is taking. If she were dwelling on the wider level she would not manage to study. The cosmic level is so much vaster, it includes this life and many others. The level of the physical body is concerned with daily life, in fact with everything that has to do with life, such as exams, driving a car, relationships, working, gathering knowledge, being happy with a little compliment . . .

As she herself puts it: 'The one level is like a big arch and the other is one drawer in it.'

Is this spirituality? It is, at least, clear 'knowing'.

I saw a woman on television who had been in prison for ten years in Malaysia, for smuggling drugs, in all ignorance, for a friend she trusted. Rancour, devastation, sorrow and immeasurable fear. Death cell. Everything. That woman had gone through hell. It was striking how her eyes shone, how gentle and soft she looked. She told how in that prison, slowly but surely, she had started once again to see the beauty of things. A sunbeam, a colour, a smile. She had started to focus on this and her heart had opened up to people, people in general. She said the bad is part of it too, everything in the prison and how people had ended up there. But the other is equally there. The pain was transformed into love. A kind of forgiveness.

We can't all do this. But I think it is precisely this that steps to freedom are about. Knowing the pain is there, in everybody, and in the end, someday, feeling affection for the pain and the curious choices of others.

How annoying that it sounds so goody-goody when it is about fundamentals. The oppressiveness of 'the true faith' makes you hardly dare talk about that kind of thing. The difference is, I think, in the message that you have to love your fellow human being and thereby leave yourself out. For loving yourself is not allowed. Being there for others, yes. But can't you only do this if you love yourself? The more you forgive yourself, love yourself, the more you have it in you to give. The more you switch on your little lights the more you are able to aim your rays where you consider it necessary.

'God' has been cut down to human-size. Surrounded with rules and laws and explanations and sin, a human is little or nothing, bonded to the never-to-be-erased all-encompassing original sin. Well, yes, that cuts you down to size.

Luckily there is more than just measure to human-size. A woman rediscovers the beautiful without the Bible and without seeing 'the light'. She saw a small sunbeam, a beam of the sun itself. Not like: God was in that small beam and then she was saved and so on. No, the sun. Part of something so beautiful that she saw more and more beauty. *That* she was herself, she was part of that beauty. Her own light surfaced and was still shining out two years later through the television.

'It's about an attitude to life,' says my son.

'The one level is like a big arch and the other is a drawer within it,' says my daughter.

Energy is welling up in me. Happy, happy with life. Connected with the earth, with my body. Body and earth are the same, nothing more than dust. But as long as there is life in it, it is marvellous to be alive.

Come into my garden! Listen! Here around me the place is full of chatter, chirping, crackling, shaking and blowing. Here all life dances in its own rhythm on the gentle breeze of time. Grows, blossoms, withers and dies. All kinds of groups of birds clamour together, doing their own thing. Yet the bird talk forms a harmony. And so do the trees, the plants, the flowers. The garden is not a wild one but laid out on old ground, finding in it not only a new way but also its own. We are stupid when we think we can handle life on our own while there is so much sweetness and support around us. But then, if you don't see it or want to see it . . . The trouble is that we are no longer able to see it.

Aeroplanes fall on houses. Wars are destroying whole cultures while other cultures still in their infancy are being shaken by turbulent historical shifts, people are powerless in the face of human violence. My other daughter says: 'That's part of it, Mum, it's a survival instinct.'

Now that I talk more with the sun and receive the craziest answers I understand it; that time in the car when the sun said I didn't have to be alone any more, firstly it was a true answer, and secondly the sun has never left me alone since then. I realise too that the answer might have something to do with the following story. Just listen.

'Hallo sun.'
'Hallo.'
'Do you have something to tell me?'
'If you have something to ask.'

Panting and puffing I go and sit on a stone on my way down after climbing about 900 metres. Around me thousands of flowers grow in every possible colour, a little brook ripples gently and reassuringly. As if everything is perfect. And it is. But what the sun said next was too crazy!

Okay, here goes: 'How do I get rid of this headache while climbing?'
'Simply practise.'
'Just continue?'
'Yes.'
'Up to and including climbing the Jungfrau?' (It is 4158 metres high.)
'No.'
'Like today is okay?'
'Yes, but not alone.'
'What do you mean not alone, my friend. I like to walk with friends but if I *am* alone I don't have a choice and that's okay for me too.'
'Not alone.'
'Well, with whom then?'
'With me.' Unbelievable! And what lightness and sense of humour.

It is now half past seven and the sun is almost gone. I have to hurry so we can still walk down together!

'Hey, sun, I'm walking with you! But I can't look at you, you are too bright for me . . .'

'I'll supply a little cloud.' While I carry on walking I kind of think I must have thought this up myself, but a bit later a little cloud does appear! Every time we exchange a few sentences I stop, open my little purple backpack on the first flat stone I find, zip open, notepad out, and quickly start writing. To avoid inventing things at second hand. It's really amusing. And: 'Yes, it's hard having two legs when you want to go down such a steep mountain path of grit and stones. But equally it's very enjoyable to be human. You experience the craziest things and all kinds of stuff that makes having two legs worthwhile. Even if now they are knocked up from the long walk,' I go on chattering to the sun.

I felt very protected today on my walk through the high mountains and glaciers. The brooks and waterfalls caused me a lot giggling and wriggling too. Great fun. So wonderful not to be cut off. Being together with all this sparkling life around me. The sun pulled some little clouds across itself in the heat of the day, so that it wouldn't be too much. Later in the day, when it was cooler, she came out again. The wind has also been very kind to me. There was a soft breeze all the time and I think that the little cloud played along by slipping in front of the sun just then . . . An excellent cooperation of the elements. It was all there again!

Today it surely proved to be an advantage to walk without friends.

The next walk I take a few days later with two women friends. It is a beautiful day with a radiant blue sky and a soft summer breeze. After walking for a few hours we are close to the top of a mountain pass. The girls are tired. It is their first day here in the mountains. I have a terrible urge to go and look over the pass and decide to go on alone. Straight across the meadows, steeply upwards. Each time I think I'm there, there's another hill. Further and further I go, I can no longer stop or rest, I have to get up there. A mist forms in front of my eyes, a kind of climbing fever takes hold of me. Then suddenly I become aware of the wind. A hard, dry wind that constantly tugs at me. Is the weather changing? Should I look around me to see whether I can go further? Is there a storm or a tempest coming? In this way the wind shakes me out of my stubborn one-pointedness and I see that the sun is no longer shining. Hey, if the sun isn't there any more, am I perhaps doing something wrong? We were going to walk together! Looking up I see that it is at least a full half-hour to the pass. I feel how tensely I have been walking, my face is beetroot red from effort. It's getting late, my friends are waiting down below in the meadow and I can of course climb the pass another time via the usual path. What was I doing? I turn around and walk downwards. Ten steps further on the sun reappears and that day she does not go away again. My imagination?

For the first time after a high climb I don't have a headache that night. Not my imagination.

Summer ends with a very nasty experience. A tragic and in that moment unavoidable misunderstanding with a person very dear to me. It made me sick and miserable, I could hardly look out of my eyes. The very last day I'm alone again and I can't leave Switzerland without a last walk and precisely to that mountain pass. Despite my thumping head and the pain in my stomach I pack my rucksack with water and sandwiches and take the car to the other side of the valley. I drive up the winding, sandy, stone-strewn little track and leave the car there at the foot of the mountain. This time I take the usual mountain path and once up there I sit down gasping and enjoying the incredible view. I see the mountain tops stretching into the endless distance on both sides of the pass. I eat a bit, lie down and close my eyes. When I open them again, there in the middle of the mountains above the pass an 'angel' comes towards me in the form of an old man. He has been on the

highest summits and takes me back down. He is happy when
I laugh, 'For you have to leave Switzerland joyfully!' he says.
As if he knew . . .

Every word we exchanged was valuable. Once below he
held me for a moment, he said that we both needed this. The
only cars by the shepherds' huts amongst the cows were ours
standing cheek by cheek. Each facing in opposite directions.

The invisible energies work that way too.

When I was a child, 'outside' was a haven, a blessing. A necessity for my mental balance. I didn't know then that nature was
giving me of her energies, I received unknowingly.

And now, now I go and sit and ask the sun who is showing
herself today: 'What shall I write about?' and I hear: 'Yourself.'

I understand that by writing about my slow and yet inten-
sive process, I can clarify how the more honestly you confront
yourself, the more deeply you can connect with nature.

Naturally people can be connected with nature in very different ways, via a dog, a cat, birds and all the other animals
we can have in the house. Others are completely unconsciously
in contact in their own way. The only thing they miss out on
is the dialogue and thereby the knowledge of the presence of
that dimension. The exchange. Maybe it doesn't matter. It's
about what you are looking for. The lamas in the Himalayan
mountains live in complete indifference to the world outside
their direct surroundings. Their seeming indifference is nothing more than a 'staying non-involved'. They are engaged with
other things. Their harmony and their vitality are their contribution to the world. Whether they enjoy life I don't know of
course but their simple, clear lifestyle contributes to the positive energy. How can you live in the world of humans, taking
part in it, and simultaneously be part of the world of spirit and
take part in that?

My conscious choice to confront life, the earth in all its mater-
iality, arose at Martha's. Precisely through my body I want to
be connected with the metaphysical aspect of life, with the

essence of things. My curiosity about what lies behind things has sharpened the antennae which bring me ever closer to the essence. Naturally there have been times when I have yearned for the tranquillity of seclusion but I have never truly stepped out of the world in order to connect in true solitude with the All. I find life far too pleasant and you simply cannot deny the world as it is. That's just not what it's all about in my view. So my choice was in fact made a long time ago: I want to be part of both worlds. In other words, the full life of a human being who decided to incarnate. Experiencing both body and spirit with full consciousness in the reality of the present-day world. I want to link the two realities in an integrated way, consciously. My life-path with all those thousands of great and small decisions has led me to this. 'Sacred non-attachment,' warned the old clairvoyant woman who saw that I too was going to pieces over the misery of the world. No, my place is not in a cloister; it is precisely this baffling world and worldly things that I love. Nor would I like to be with the lamas, even though they are so clearly engaged with life amidst and with that wonderful nature. Nor is it my way to have out-of-body spiritual experiences, which many 'spirit-full' people do. They are able to travel out of their body and other such fantastic things. With me it is about the connection with essences, the essential core of things, *in* the world, in my body. From there I can have the most fascinating experiences, as far away as need be. Why else did I choose to incarnate? But how do you 'live' that connection? It doesn't make it any easier. An either/or choice which kept me busy for a while: first on the one side with politics, feminism, the peace movement (to name just a few areas of controversy), and later on the other side with spiritual discoveries and experiences. That choice no longer makes sense to me. For me it is and/and. An equilibrium between two realities.

I go and sit quietly and open myself to my greater consciousness. I ask: 'How shall I carry on from here?' The answer is: 'Live in connectedness with *all* the elements around you, the visible as well as the invisible.' Once more I am aware of the context in which this answer is given and I understand that it is only possible through trial and error, with all my question marks and my human duality. It isn't situated between the spirit and the world, but between the darkness and the light, including the shadow sides in between. In other words: between being connected and disconnected, in communication or out of communication with the light of life.

The centre. Which centre? My centre which I lose regularly. There I go again, full speed, headlong into a rotten mood.

And then I see that little wisp of a child huddled up in the kitchen, miserable because of the quarrel which I have started with someone on the phone, and my heart melts. After a few more convulsions I crawl with difficulty back into my centre and as a reasonable being I debate with — there is no one else here for the moment — myself. It is of course ridiculous what that woman wants but I cannot impose my choices on the children. Let them go their own way, they are old enough to use their own eyes and if they make a 'mistake', as I myself so often do, then that is their lesson. Accept the shadow side, girl, your own and the children's in all their choices.

When I visualise my severe reaction as if it were a human figure (a method to get clear about yourself that I was trained in during my course on intuition and whereby you can look at difficult situations with a certain amount of distance and in the form of images, thus lightening things up), it looks like a very stiff gentleman in a suit who greets me with a flourishing bow. To be honest he looks rather old-fashioned. I ask him why he is so severe and whether he is still in tune with me; as answer he turns into a porcupine. That feels better. A small, on my part venomous, stab to indicate my boundaries can do no harm. And maybe I'll add a bit of poison just once. I continue my visualisation and ask the reasonable part of myself what it looks like in reduced but human form. Well, that looks like a Mum behind the teapot. Forever patient and understanding, she is always there for everybody, just a touch self-sacrificing. Outwardly she looks like her teapot, round, goody-goody, unchanging. Imagine there was no link to my ex-gentleman in dress-coat, what an unattainable example that would be for my children to follow.

How can I describe all that I experience? Am I standing on my head or am I different the other way round? The world looks so different. I drive along the dike, the sun is shining low on the water, big unwieldy barges are sailing in the middle of the river. One low and full of cargo, the other lying high in the water, empty. On both sides of the dark bow the foam shapes itself like the moustache of a dandy in a tuxedo, the sharp front end in between looking like a nose.

What am I doing on this earth for heaven's sake? What am I here for, what am I for, for what am I? For myself, for the river, for the sun, for the earth? Part of the earth, that I am sure of, more and more. I feel the substance of it, the closeness of all that belongs with it. Feet in the earth, that too ever more firmly. Sometimes I feel more like a little sister of the earth and everything that grows on it than of human beings. The road winds over the dike, the birds fly low over the land, a child with a backpack is riding home on a moped from school. I don't know any more, it is so different now, now that I am closer to you, dear trees, dear flowers, clouds, sun, brother wind, sister water. One thing is for sure, the land here offers endless space . . . The sun shines over far horizons with a pale autumn light. There is grazing in the lush meadows, croaking in the ditches. Two beautifully coloured cock-pheasants who have escaped the guns stand proudly at the side of this little road. Blues, grey-blues, greys, yellows, yellow-blues. reddish autumn colours, green.

The bunkers from the war still stand in the landscape to remind us. Why do children get to see so many violent films? A delicious smell of food comes wafting to me from a farm. My body is asking for a new way of eating and drinking. Different but how? It is because I invited the nature-energies to enter straight into my body. Because of the heightened sensitivity to very subtle energies I have been working with all this time. Now it proves to require an adjustment I don't know how to handle very well. I keep off coffee, and meat. I try this and then that. I discover that it is more about appreciating the value of the food than about following a certain diet. An awareness of the vitality in the different elements of food. Didn't the Ancient Peoples do likewise? Not chewing food while talking. Respect for my own body, the same respect I show the earth, or vice versa. Only eating what is really nutritious. When I reflect that there is light in all the little cells, even of tomatoes and beans, then I want to eat whatever contains the most light. What I mean is that a tomato ripened in a greenhouse has, of course, less light in it than the tomato that grew in open sunlight and soft rain. Actually you can see how much light there is in different kinds of food. One simply radiates more brightly than the other! Now that we know from all the research into the emotional life of plants* how they react to loving attention, tomatoes that have been grown with care and attention are naturally the most radiant! We need each other's radiance. It is pure food for your body *and* for your own light. Vital energy. Everything that comes forth from healthy earth, ripened in those sunbeams. The life-juices flow into my life-juices, in contrast to the dead energy of food that does not contain light. Earlier on in this book I wrote about Dr Popp and his discovery of biophotons, the laser beams that transmit information. Thus it is too that the information my body receives from the living tomato is healthy, vital information for all my cells, while the hothouse plants transmit dull, joyless information. What happens to your body when all you eat is fast-food? What kind of information gets transmitted? I can't bear to think about it! Just changing that in your life will undoubtedly have enormous consequences!

When I cook, I give attention to the food.

Attention and love are keywords to light the inner light.

I feel like dancing. The little ferry is crossing the water, it is a quarter to five. In an hour I have to go and cook for my hungry children. That routine is no longer at all to my liking. I want to cook as part of the rhythm of the dance, my dance of life. I

---

* See Peter Tompkins/Christopher Bird, *The Secret Life of Plants*, Penguin, London, 1975.

want to sail across on the little ferry for pleasure without rushing, without obligations waiting for me and pushing me on.

Choices, choices, always choices. And that is one of them. I am writing for the sake of writing, just for myself and to share all this beauty. I think this is the purpose. The more people tell what they know and experience of the metaphysical world, the more attainable this reality becomes. If this is being read by someone who is concerned with the same things and through this book is getting precisely the support they need to continue, for at the moment it is still a rather lonely road, then I write also for that reason. Not so much to be understood. Nor is there a holy voice which is giving me the task of writing all this. I want it myself. This deep need to share with others what I experience. To tell that the superficial is not the only reality.

And if you have ended up having the same experiences, don't tell me about it! Live it! Experience it! Tell people around you and find your own way in it.

The emanation you see of the healthy tomato, just like your own inner radiation which exists around you, is the fine energy that is called the aura. When you are able to sense it, and this we all can learn to do if we feel like it, you discover that through its clarity you get a feeling about that tomato or that person. In the case of humans, our thoughts are inscribed in our aura. These attract similar thoughts and the people who go with them. Every aura has its individual frequency and vibration, its individual rhythm. Because everyone and everything is unique. Each cell housing that little moving light is in constant renewal. In just the same way there is a kind of culture-rhythm that belongs to your environment, your country. You generally feel good in it, probably because your own rhythm has attuned itself to it. From birth onwards you have been able to adapt to it. Someone from another culture not only has a different auric vibration of their own but also another culture-rhythm and it is often difficult to maintain your own frequency *and* feel good in a culture-frequency which is not your original one. Very often you constrict your own rhythmic radiation or you abandon it altogether. In other words you take a defensive position or you adapt. It is truly very difficult to maintain your auric vibration in an open, natural way in an environment that does not match it. As such I have met a great many people whose auras were so delicate that it looked as if they were ill. What was happening, if you look at it in a different way, was that they weren't able to live with their frequency in the harshness of the city, the pollution, and so on. When you are different from the lowest common denominator you are punished right away with a label which generally boils down to your not being 'normal'. The only way out of this dilemma, in my experience, is to convince yourself that you are positively normal. Yet again another decision, namely about accepting differences or the desire for everybody to be the same.

Through all the years that I have been free of all those norms and rituals of my surroundings and culture, I feel that I have found peace. That I am happy with myself and with what I see. And I end up at the original vibration of my aura, the one I was born with and which I too have slowly been adapting to the lowest common denominator. A certain lightness and airiness which had lain hidden beneath the weight of responsibility and the duties. Right now my aura is filled with vital energy, an openness towards the nature beings, dancing, painting, writing, enjoying an active life with new goals.

In this way I am meeting people who have also ended up in an enjoyment phase, who are using their time for 'being' and are finding this the meaning of their life. So a bit less 'doingness'. People who think it worthwhile to live the way they want and feel what is good for them and what agrees with them. Finding a place where they can fully be themselves to develop further, to grow. There are people who make a conscious choice to work less hard, to take a part-time job. More and more work is being shared of necessity and quite by chance people are getting more opportunity to plan their own time. In our Calvinistic little country, not working is considered the mother of vice. But a full-time job, which in my experience can be just as wonderful, is indeed a different kind of enjoyment from what I am talking about here. What I am talking about is a conscious choice sometime in your life to take a different stand, to live differently. To build in a certain amount of rest whereby you get a greater opportunity to feel and listen, and to create space within your working week to send your head on a bit of a holiday. As ever, it involves choices once more. Sometimes it doesn't look like a choice, yet it is. That may sound easy; it isn't. You can allow your circumstances to determine your life or you create your own circumstances. It is possible that precisely through this you avoid a part of yourself. It's a hard process and often a struggle. I myself did it in phases. From a full-time job in an instructive environment I consciously worked towards having more rest. My body pointed out to me that I didn't give enough space to the natural in myself and on that path back to my whole self nature was an important help and teacher. I am there where I like to be. What a delightful, personally created privilege! A very old friend says: 'A time will come when people will ask you what you do and then you will answer: "I do nothing, I am."' I'm quite expert at doing; I'm training to become expert in just being.

From my diary: A lot of spinner dolphins in the bay! Flippers and snorkel on. We are swimming out at six o'clock. The water is still quite cold and the tension is building. I admit I am a bit scared of these big animals who are on home ground and in their own element while I am not a real water person. On top of that I have never before swum in the Pacific Ocean and it is big and deep! While we are swimming out into that endless ocean, suddenly they are there in my besnorkelled field of vision. Ten, twenty, no forty-seven of them, including little ones . . . Tension and fear immediately disappear and give way to a sensation of tranquillity and total confidence. Below me I see how the first rays of the sun are focused on one spot. In it the dolphins are swimming around, wonderfully beautiful in the underwater silence. Time passes, doesn't exist any more. Only this quietness with the big beings there in the grey-blue twilight. From the deep two of them surface slightly in front of me. I swim towards them, they are waiting for me, one looks at me out of the corner of his eye, very close by. All I can say is: 'Hallo, hallo, hallo' . . . I feel so close and inspired. It is exciting and new and I watch and watch and feel. Thinking is impossible now, that will come later. Imagine, I am swimming in the OCEAN! With DOLPHINS! This is not a fairy tale but really and truly reality. Limitless, endless love slowly filters through to me. I pick it up, swim amidst and with that wonderful gift and those powerful bodies, and relish the playfulness and the joy they radiate. It must have been for an hour or two that we swam there together like that.

During a breakfast under the palm trees I shared my stories with the others. With Joan who swims with the dolphins every day, counts and studies them, writes down their spiritual messages and published them in a book*, two other woman-friends and me. I feel full of energy and joy, as if I and everything around me is full of a radiant light. Is the energy, the vibration of the dolphins that high? One hour later I'm dead tired. They have effectively done something to my energy system. Thus I swim with dolphins for a whole month at six in the morning and each day something happens from which I learn.

Naturally you can also simply swim and play with dolphins and enjoy it intensely. But when you listen and feel with your full awareness there is so much more they can and want to give you. It requires a sensitivity we are all able to come up with to

---

*See Joan Ocean, *Dolphin Connection: Interdimensional Ways of Living,* Dolphin Connection, 1989.

something 'different' from the expected and familiar. Just as the music of Stockhausen, for instance, takes you into completely unknown territory because he abandons tonality. Contact with this opens up other parts of the store of information we carry with us from former lives and experiences. And it puts an even bigger smile on your face and you feel that you are alive. Dolphins are beings who make connections between heaven and earth. It looks as if they *consciously* transform light into sound. They bring light, which is pure energy, into connection with sound, which is matter. They are of course not unique in this but what is specific to dolphins is how they use the water cover of the earth as a formidable conductor to connect cosmic energies with the energy of this planet Earth. They themselves seemingly act as the transformer and the fact that they are in water makes this possible. They know where people are swimming and they find you straight away if they feel like it. We all know the stories about dolphins saving people. That we can learn an awful lot from dolphins is indeed clear. At the moment they are teaching me how you can communicate in images. They pick up your thought-forms as images and send images in return. Pictures. Actually, just as in a laser show pictures are projected into space, we do likewise with our thoughts which the animals and the trees and the plants then pick up. In precisely the same way they return their 'answer'. We can catch these in images or in words which we hear resonating inside us.

Currently more and more people are getting into dialogue with dolphins. We each do this in our own way via imagery. Seemingly dolphins are in a continuous alpha-state. This is a deep level of relaxed awareness which you reach in meditation and from which you have a wider-than-usual perception because human-created boundaries fall away. It is interesting that a growing number of people meditate and practise this wider awareness. This could be why a remarkably large number of people communicate with dolphins, or at least want to be in their vicinity, and why dolphins so often appear in dreams. In this relaxed state you connect more easily with your surroundings.

We lost a paddle from the kayak while we were swimming and didn't notice it. Dolphins are swimming past. A row of six, seven bent little fins, one neatly behind the other in undulating motion. A bit further on and right behind them something black is floating, the paddle! It looks like a game to them. Together with Joan I swim with two bottle-nosed dolphins. They are playing underwater with a plastic bag like we would with a ball. One lets go and the other catches. So the four of us played 'plastic bag' for a couple of minutes in the light of the sunbeams underwater and in that delightful soundlessness in which only the high tones of the animals are audible. Images of my most tender childhood surface irresistibly: one and the same light through the bars of my little bed, soft colours and a peaceful tranquillity, safety. Wondrous how these animals spread peace, safety and love around them. Then early one morning I have a contact with one bigger male dolphin.

There underwater I shamelessly told him everything about myself and asked him for advice. Not as a therapist but as a very wise being. Once again I get a unique answer which I couldn't have thought up myself. I want to tell something of it.

To my question about how I should proceed with all that I presently know about the contact we humans can have with the life-forms in nature and about the contact they have with spaces in the cosmos, whether I have to throw myself in the deep end by writing about it, meaning going public with it, I got to hear: 'You never have to be afraid any more. Never, not of anything. Stay in this path of energy. You will receive everything.' I heard it over and over again until it became an echo underwater. Everything, everything . . . and then I dived down behind the dolphin as deep as I could as a commitment to *trusting* that I will receive everything . . . It was as if a path of energy came towards me. Afterwards I felt free, sensual and snug as in a hot bath at home. To conclude, I received a shower of bubbles as healing.

The next day a lot of sadness surfaces. 'You will receive everything.' Oh, I have done my absolute best in life. My absolute best. These days the dolphins are saying: 'Shit it out!'

and show me how by pooing and peeing exuberantly in my face; thank God I have got the mask!

Well, here it goes then: I felt abandoned during my marriage and my divorce, I have started anew again and again, alone, alone an awful lot . . . I . . . how must I trust when people let me down . . . how can I simply receive everything when I have had to fight so hard to go my own way . . . it's not possible, that's not the way things work. 'Shit it out!' 'Accept!' The shit of duality, the shit of human impotence. Your own blindness and impotence.'

After a day of pain and disappointment, there outside by the patient swell of the ocean a butterfly flies over me. Time after time, transformation.

The dolphins bring us back into balance. Dolphin, you show me worlds I didn't know. Are they in your thoughts, do you live in them, are you connected with them and do I thus pick up your images? Transformation, communication, making connections, balance, all this in unconditional love, are the words I connect with you. When much later I read books that tell of experiences with dolphins and how interaction with them changed the lives of all these people, then this confirms my own experience that they also have the power of direct communication on a personal level through which the individual can change. I myself am touched by this profound contact to the deepest layers of my being and am fundamentally transformed by it.

I come into contact with how everything is put together with so much love. Or rather I should say: everything is put together with so much love. Out there by the water I feel the beam of light that hangs above the bay and the love that emanates from it fills me. Sirius? I read in several books that the dolphins are connected with this star and with all the force-fields associated with it. How do people know this? Do I have to link up with it?

Yesterday a big group. They came and got us and surrounded us. They looked at me too and were swimming so close by that I could have collided with them. Felt so much like touching one. Eyes, noses, fins, bodies. Hallo, hallo, hallo! We see each other, eyes meet, sonars feel and scan. Because I lack sonar, I open all my senses and focus myself on receiving something, whatever it might be, but probably something unknown and unexpected. Again I take joy in the beautiful strong bodies, the control of their physical strength. With their precise, measured movements they waste a minimum of energy. In the tail I see reflections of the rainbow. Three times I reach out my hand. Each time the dolphin swims away just a bit with an almost imperceptible movement of the tail, so I don't succeed. Clearly these intelligent, free mammals are not to be touched. Only in captivity, in dolphinariums, is this possible but generally not 'in the wild'. *If* an opportunity to touch a dolphin presents itself, it will only be possible at the instigation of the dolphin itself. Respect is necessary, certainly with regard to these magnificent creatures.

Time stands still there underwater. I lose myself in the blue, the sunbeams which play and entice me like the dolphins deep, deep into the deep. I could stay there . . . it is so very beautiful, yes, that temptation is there for sure. Maybe because of the timelessness, the light that dances and plays. Isn't it the same transparent blue colour we knew before we incarnated in our bodies and which we will see again before long? . . . If in this moment I were to dissolve there in all that blue of the Pacific Ocean, filled with the dolphins' unconditional love, it would be very easy and simple. Who knows, I may really do this for split seconds, for sometimes I have the feeling I'm not there any more, no longer know where I am. Again that feeling of timelessness you get down there. An experience of being in the future, present and past all at once.

Time-less — no time — outside of time. Floating, diving, rolling, flowing in the soft water and in the playfulness and phenomenal communication of these strength-giving creatures.

And so the first morning of my next visit to the island and the ocean I swam with eight dolphins. They were floating very slowly beneath me and I heard very clearly: 'Make contact.' A big man was swimming in my vicinity, he was fanatically trying to get close to the animals and didn't notice at all that there was another human body bobbing around. I took off my swimming mask and said, 'Hallo,' but of course he didn't hear me. So I waited till he put his head above water and then it worked. But in the following days I understood that it was about making contact with everyone I met during this time on the island. I was giving a workshop there and maybe, because I was focused on the work, I had made myself less open to others. But now I had received that message very clearly. Consequently the contacts that took place were deep and useful and in effect caused me to write this book! Thank you dolphins! Writing a book about my experiences is not interesting so much because it is about my experiences but because, through expressing our spiritual experiences and insights and our life path towards them, we stimulate each other and thus a new consciousness grows and becomes a stronger energy field. I also want to tell loudly and clearly that there is more than the human form of communication, that there is more than the visible, that there is unimaginably more than the material side of life. Just as this book hasn't appeared only out of my head but out of my whole being. And that is precisely the only way to enter into a dialogue with all that lives around us. So many people have similar experiences but think they are alone in it.

In the meantime, there underwater I hear high tones like far echoes coming out of the dark depths and there is exuberant playing. My energy system yet again gets an enormous boost by swimming close to the dolphins. It is one big togetherness party. Playing together. Not so much answer and question this time but rather a total communication of being.

Never ever have I swum so closely with them, in all respects . . . I am allowed to be part of this group and feel accepted into their pod aura. Side by side we swim. First admitted into the pod, then between two dolphins, I get taken further and further out of the bay. A kind of energy stream keeps me connected to these two. They wait for me. Then they too split up and after some hesitation I follow the male for he seems to be looking at me and I think he wants to take me with him. He brings me back into the bay. After swimming for a long time I notice I'm being taken around in a circle. I don't understand what he is trying to get across to me . . . I keep asking: 'What do I need to understand?' Circle after circle we draw. 'What . . . ?' No answer. Finally I look down at the sea bed, which is visible here, full of corals. And yes, below me the seven-pointed star of whitish and greyer coral . . . I know this spot, I have been brought here three times now. It is a healing spot. In that moment of recognition I am sent an intense flow of love and the next moment the animal is gone. All at once, completely. What do I do with this star? For a time I hovered above it, looked at it, took the image of the star into my heart and let a firework of stars tumble and dance through me, as a confirmation yet again of my decision to continue. Very light I swim back through the sunbeams in the clear underwater blue. In love. In love with life, light, water, with the possibilities that exist. In love with the love in all of life that gives unconditionally and helps me and everyone to aspire to a life of joy and good.

I read: the seven-pointed star links the triangle with the square and is considered the music of the spheres, the harmony of the world, humankind in its full power. Seven! Yes, that also means the totality of the universe in motion. I know that I am connected with the seven-pointed star. It has helped me through the most difficult moments in my life, imbuing me with the realisation that everything changes. For change means life.

Back on the shore I continue reflecting on it, focusing on the star. I hear, 'Heal the bay,' and understand that we humans, as a link in the chain of life, have to do our part. I must not feel inferior to the power in the other life around me, like now the dolphins with their intelligence, healing qualities and spiritual capacities. And, because I too have healing power, I have to use this power and act. Every little bit helps. From my bed there behind the mosquito net looking out over the water I have healed the bay.

Every human being is good at something that another

person or another life-form is not able to do. Together we can do quite a lot and if we are open to the potential of all that lives, we can work together magnificently. That day I promised myself to direct my healing powers towards the earth too and to help increase the contact between humankind and earth.

There are quite a lot of people who give earth-healing, do resonance therapies and suchlike. I want to do my humble bit for it in my way.

A black crab slides very carefully towards the water, unsuspecting of all this philosophising. On the other side of the road somebody is building a house with quite a lot of drilling and sawing noise. A jet full of passengers flies over the bay towards its destination.

I feel beautiful, light, transparent. Delicate, light-giving, radiant. As if in every cell a spark of golden light has entered. A rebirth. Part of the hibiscus, the plumeria, the wind, the water, the butterfly, the dolphin, the wind playing through the palm leaves. I can only lie down, not even sleep. I feel part of the gossamer structure of everything. I feel I am the movement of the mango leaf there in front of my bed. The wind that moves it, the colour. I am in that colour, in that movement. And yet I am separate, myself. Everything is terribly beautiful. The beauty of the inside is indescribable. I literally cannot find words to describe it. It is also too transparent for words. Too much essence to name it. Wondrous. I get up and go outside to be completely in nature and sitting on the little wall by the ocean I experience how it is to be able to feel straight through everything, to be subtle energy with the other, at an equal frequency, vibration . . . With the water, the waves and the spray of the surf, the lava, the grass . . . it is extraordinary . . . I sense further, yes also with the creepy eel, the teeth of the eel! The shark? Yes, that too and its jaws . . . I sense through Elizabeth, through the coconut, the rubber dinghy, the white lacquered iron chair, through plastic, my towel . . . everything. Here comes a woman paddling in a kayak, through her I *can't* sense. This means there are after all certain energies which are not clear enough to feel through. Interesting and very exciting this! It feels delightful, so light and at one. I'm not spacey, I'm not out of my body. I'm just plain me and I have my wits about me. I'm hungry and go and eat a thick tomato sandwich.

One day before leaving this extraordinary place of learning on earth I swim and come across a small group of dolphins with a youngster. They don't feel like communicating and are swimming deep below me in a kind of meditative state. Probably they are simply digesting their tasty meal.

I say: 'Hey, come on, tomorrow is my last day, I'm leaving. I have received so much from you, don't need anything else, I only want to play.' The young dolphin slowly turns around, looks upwards and with one strong beat of her tail joins me. Bending her body from right to left, upwards, downwards, and then she jumps at breakneck speed out of the water! I follow her in all her movements except the last one . . . She watches me all the time with a very open eye and even turns her head so far towards me that little wrinkles appear on the side of her neck. This too is a new experience. We have real fun together. Then, when someone else joins us, she leaves.

The last day I paddle out in the kayak into the dead calm bay, into the early morning. It looks as if we are all alone. Elizabeth swims out next to the kayak and I will swim back. There are no dolphins in sight, but a lot of jellyfish. They are the ones like threads, often you do not see them, especially when you swim against the light. I'm annoyed that these things are there, after so much beauty, turning our — my — last swimming pleasure into irritation. And when I swim straight into a big knot of jellyfish thread, I swear underwater and say aloud that I don't want to leave here like this, in disharmony with the water. After that I let go of the irritation and: *I saw no more jellyfish!*

'You will receive everything . . .' Yes but what is my next step? How can I plan my new direction? With whom? I go and sit quietly in a timeless state of consciousness, by emptying myself, putting my thoughts away for a while. I am getting better and better at this simply by practising. This gives me a much wider awareness, just like before underwater. Thus I can ask a question of my larger self (sometimes called 'higher self' but I feel in this a tendency to hierarchy), which is connected with a much broader reservoir of information, another level. The question arises in me: 'Why am I living now?'

'To feel part of all life on earth.

To be part of everything.

To have fun.'

'What for?'

'You know already. It is good that you awaken it again.

For the joy, the fun.

To make others feel this, to demonstrate this.

To heal yourself. Not to be afraid any more.

To fuse together.'

'Does this lead to a purpose?' asks my Calvinistic background.

'Be the being of light that you are. Be light, light, light. It leads to connections.

Make connections.

Feel connections.

Discover them and be the connection.'

'Any precise purpose?' I cannot help it . . .

And all at once the answer comes, remarkably in English: 'Make yourself humble and feel, breathe, overcome your fear and be our ambassador.'

Well . . . that is quite something. 'How?'

'By feeling.'

Oh yes, that I can understand better. But:

'What do I do with the misery of the world, the hardness, the mess, and . . . ?'

'Love.'

'Yes, I know that, those people like Martin Luther King, Gandhi . . .'

'Yes.'

'So?'

'Don't worry about negative outcomes, remain in your heart, be yourself.
What matters is the light, open yourself up to it and laugh! Don't fix anything. Don't count on people, houses, securities. Trust.
Trust in the power of everything around you.
Learn to receive. Trust and receive. Be a link.
You are a guiding star, pass it on!'
The star at the bottom of the ocean . . .

When I was flying back home and watching the last light of a long day through the aeroplane's little window, I 'saw' and felt the enormous love-energy that hangs like a low net above our earth. To actually see it was quite a shock. This energy is simply there to accompany us, just like that, and I have never seen it before. With this as well, all you have to do is attune yourself to it and you will be able to feel it. It is hard to believe all the things we don't notice. Time. Rest. Openness regarding unexpected, unsuspected energy. It's all there. When I shut myself off from this connectedness, the uncertainties, the fear, the doubts start to hit me. Am I able to . . . is it possible . . . am I good . . . enough . . . ? I feel small in the face of the immense world and universe, and quite rightly so. But as soon as I connect with the cosmic whole the uncertainty is gone and I know a lot more than I am able to know on my own. Part of a whole. Connection. It makes me joyful and energetic. I feel one can be connected to an endless source of love and information. I positively did my homework for this but just as you 'forget' the grammar of a language once you know it, likewise you forget what you did to learn to make this connection and you just enjoy the results. What this homework is I find hard to say, my life I think. And what came before. 'God is never late' . . . We work our own miracles but not alone, not cut off from the totality of connections. Otherwise it isn't really a miracle.

Back home I run through the meadows straight to the waters of the river Lek. I have a strong desire to be by the water with which I have formed such a solid friendship. The river flows smooth and calm. I crouch down just at the edge of the brown water and stretch out my hands towards it. Inside I say, 'Hallo water everywhere in the world,' and the water moves towards my hands as a hallo in return. I look up to see what has moved it. There is no boat in sight, there is no wind. I feel myself flush, and moved I stay put for a while.

Amongst the masses of people, many with dull eyes, it is amazing to see how many here and there in the world have discovered their inner lights and switched them on. It happens everywhere: in prison, in the middle of a war or in our easygoing little country. Through, despite, from the dark. They radiate like angels and you find them in all professions and age groups. Whether it be a painter or a carpenter, a garden designer or a doctor. They radiate something like gentleness and certainty. They are open to the magical moments in life. They feel and see in a way which goes beyond what is immediately obvious, beyond cynicism and a future in the three-dimensional world. It looks as if we have entered a time of spiritual acceleration and are growing towards a totally different dimension of awareness. It is so very remarkable how many youngsters in the last thirty years have been born like this, with their lights on, and don't have to go the long way around by which my generation had to go to turn on our switch. They are in open contact with their own higher information. A broad information with which they can make larger connections and more easily remain free of the filtered three-dimensional information that dulls and is incomplete. To find their kindred spirits is not always easy and these youngsters often feel strange, for they are 'different'. Are we facing a turnaround?

Everywhere I go people say the most unexpected things which amaze me and make my heart jump for joy. Greater overviews, multidimensional insights. People are getting more in contact with the more subtle energies in themselves and around them, the angels, the invisible beings who are with us, protect us or learn from our experiences. People think differently about dying and former lives. The learning process we are engaged in as souls here on earth.

To what end? I think, to contribute to the growth process of all that lives in the cosmos. As the human species we certainly are no more than the mouse or the butterfly and surely no more than the ant. Nor are we less. Each life form can do something the others cannot. We are one whole. And on this earth we cannot live without each other's contribution. In Part Two of this book I talk about some of the experiences of participants in the various workshops I have given with the theme 'Dialogue with Nature', and I go deeper into the answers people have received to the question of what special task each life form has and humankind's place as a species in this. More and more people are open to the meaning of the events that happen to them. They make associations between instructive experiences in their life as a soul, on the journey throughout their lives. 'Coincidences' are recognised as the right thing happening in the right moment. They themselves made this accidental happening possible.

What you give out, you draw to you. You make your own life. We live in a time when people want to express their own identity and don't adhere as quickly to institutions. We still listen nicely to our parents as before but now we want to organise our own life according to our own ideas and insights and we want to express our own thoughts more. People listen a lot more to their own original information, their intuition. We become our own guru, not — or at least less — dependent on the authority of others.

Simultaneously fundamentalism and fascism blossom as adversaries to transformation. This attitude resonates a very big NO: don't change, hold on to the old, I don't want to learn or to hear. Belonging to a group is still what counts.

Two extremes of the same thing. What we call humankind. My very own conviction is that we are growing into our spiritual connection with that higher consciousness, that ancient knowing that is in our cells. No longer cut off from the loving beings around us in the cosmos and on and in the earth. The whole plant and animal world is connected with this and radiates this unity. In this they are our teachers. The wisdom they carry can help us humans to open up our hearts and feelings again and to live life fully.

November: autumn in Switzerland. Everything is afire and aflame, with a stillness in the belly. Time to release the exuberant blossoming and quietly prepare for the coming introspection of winter. This year I don't take part in this at all. There is still exuberance in my belly. A feeling of intense pleasure underlies my words and actions, just a touch deeper, and comes across as total cheerfulness. Maybe this is the real autumn. Walking in the soft bright light of the almost-full moon, the mountains silhouetted whitely, pregnant with fresh snow, I feel once more at one with everything. The substantiality we share is so clear to me now. I am connected in body and soul. Isn't there a similar formula when you get married? It sounds very grandiose anyway, while for me it's now so natural. I don't know how to put it differently. It's wondrous to feel the coherence of myself as a human with the essences of the elements in my surroundings. It is difficult even just to put this into words, and to convey the simplicity of it is even harder.

Can this connectedness only exist when you are not connected with the hubbub of the world? Only when you stand outside of it? Free from it?

This way of living requires a certain tranquillity. In the stillness of the tranquillity you are able to make the connection. Isn't it just like a stone or a plant which naturally radiates energy but does it in far greater measure when you aim your attention at it, get in contact with it, open yourself up to it? The plant world does this quite naturally, only we humans have to decide with our brain to do it. It's about together. Doing together, talking, thinking, feeling together. Sharing the earth.

My colleague and friend Lydia asks: 'Don't you have to be very developed to get involved with these things? If I don't know there are guides, that trees can give me strength, how can I feel them, let alone talk with them?' I think this is true for people who have had an intellectual education, for a lot of their original intuition has been suppressed by the book-knowledge that has been crammed into it. I think that particularly people who didn't receive intellectual schooling can connect with nature in a very original way. Consciously or unconsciously. Precisely as I did when I was a child and most children still do. Mountain people for instance talk little; I suspect that in one way or another they are connected with everything around them. The 'real' ones know when the weather is changing, they feel it in their bodies. They 'know' it. The travelling people knew (before they were ordered to stay in predetermined locations) that they had better not park their caravan in certain spots for there were evil spirits. 'You can't sleep there at night,' they said. 'There the fire goes out while the wood is good.' 'There the horses get sick.' They were clearly in contact with their intuition which told them when there were bad energies around them. They are in touch with their creative psyche. That part of yourself with which you can visualise, with which you meditate, paint, write, feel, know . . . The instrument of your soul is your imagination . . .

My inquisitiveness about what is invisible to the three-dimensional eye, about the other reality, the metaphysical, has taken me quite far already. I know that a lot more is yet to come for there is so much more. But without mumbo-jumbo and special holy ritual, for goodness' sake. When it's like that it no longer holds any meaning for me, for then it is all about power. About knowing better, knowing more and so on.

Finally I come to life-force. In the essence of you and me, of all that lives, there is a life-elixir. The essence you find through living. Incarnated in a specific body we learn our lessons on earth, with the circumstances of duality. In this we are in the process of becoming an autonomous being. Mentally free. Free of oppression, rules and regulations, prevailing cultural patterns, authority in the guise of parents, politics, group and dogma. Free to give our very own vital essence the chance to flow at full spate. With all the unforeseen consequences of that. Today I was talking with a girl of sixteen who is going to go her own way, outside of the norms and standards of her culture. It's shocking for the parents. Why is this her path? Because in this way she is in her vital power. Because this *is* her path. It doesn't require an explanation in the form of a justification. It confirmed for me that this is exactly what it is all about, often outside of the norms. And in supreme contentment, sitting in front of the fire, I feel my body rocking delightfully. Immediately I realise it is not me doing this. I know the feeling very well . . . I'm getting a huge embrace from Zoro! Are you back or were you always present in a form I can't sense? 'That's not important,' I hear and I feel that the most important thing is to surrender to the rocking itself. How delicious life is. I can't imagine a happier moment. What more do I want from life, for heaven's sake? The same joy I know from my contact with the sun, the dolphins. I ask, now from Zoro, how it works and as answer I get that it is the same.

'How can it be?' I ask aloud.

'You have got hold of the essence.' Oh yes, that's how it is. The life-elixir, the spiral of life, is the essence in everything. Externally the forms are different but the core makes up one whole. All is one.

Somewhere there is someone who thinks the earth is going to explode.

I got in touch with my own life-elixir and through it with the essence of all living things. Light, life-energy, a drink of life for the last phase of this, my life. For eternity? I feel like it. Everything is possible in balance with nature.

PART TWO

Exercises and Examples
A Helping Hand

Contact with nature is of course just one of the paths that lead to wholeness, of yourself and of the earth, and can express itself in various ways according to your capacity, your needs, your direction. How deep the connection goes depends equally upon yourself. One person finds consolation and rest, another talks to animals, plants or trees. And then there is the possibility of opening yourself up to a dialogue with questions and answers or noticing signs that are shown to you as a kind of language, if you look for them. That's one way of better integrating your life with the life around you. *All* the life. In every case it is about a relationship with the living world around you, an exchange. A mutuality. The Ancient Peoples speak rightly about their relationship with everything. And naturally we are connected, we cannot do without each other. We have lost sight of each other too much on this side of the globe. And we are completely unaware that we can learn from this other life. Maybe for a start we shouldn't have invented concrete which literally separates our feet from the earth. Yet, even with the world as it is, we can once more connect consciously and get to know each other better. Everything in nature is patiently waiting for us. It knows and feels our vibrations. It is up to us to start living in a manner in which we are open to each other's frequencies, lessons and wisdom, in gratitude for the existence of the other.

In the workshops I give on dialogue with nature, I see how people are once more engaging with this encounter on these various levels and thereby finding paths suitable for themselves. Equally I come across the pain and sorrow that are touched by the unconditional love nature offers. Its openness, directness and honesty highlight the parts in you that are cut off. The natural life-forms, which are *not* closed down by the problems of being human, offer us a safe way to live cleanly and openly once more. It is not at all easy for us but in the end it makes us more whole and complete human beings. The exercises I use in the workshops, which are aimed at this exploration of oneself in communication with nature, I took in part from my training but mostly they have developed from my dialogue with nature. I include just a few of them in this chapter as a possible contribution to your own progress. To it I add examples of experiences and interesting information from participants — with their consent, naturally. Probably these too will contribute to a greater understanding of the path you can follow to become more at one with yourself and the life around you.

So there were two questions: What were the first messages you got *about* nature? What are the messages you are getting now *from* nature?

You can see this most easily with the help of a little meditation:

Close your eyes and direct your attention inwards. Feel your breathing. Breathe deeply and calmly. Feel how you are in contact with the earth through the soles of your feet. Take the time to feel this quietly. Now let the first messages emerge, in images or in words about nature which you as a child received from your educators, your surroundings and your culture. Through this you get an image of your first perspectives on what was considered 'nature' and how the people close around you dealt with it.

Some examples as illustration:

— 'I come from a village. We had a shop. People worked very hard. There wasn't much time to connect with nature. When I was three years old I did feel a connection with the dog. It was a dialogue. We also had pigeons, a garden. There was a lot of

work with the garden and the animals at home. My message
about nature was: hard work and taking care.

'Now the water, the wideness, gives me an enormous
amount of space. There I can breathe deliciously, and rest. The
respect I sensed for nature's own course, in Peru for instance
when I was living there, that I hadn't known and I find it very
important.'

— 'Nature simply was there. We didn't talk about it. Didn't feel
the need to go there. The garden was well taken care of but
we didn't talk about it. We clearly had respect. A tree was a living being! No devotion, absolutely not. Simply respect, rever-
ence and curiosity.

'But I have no communication, I don't receive from nature.
I don't open myself up to that. Only once, as a child of eight
or so, I was walking from one house to the next and the moon
was walking with me. That was so special, it seemed just as
if I was getting a present from that moon and I got the feeling
that I existed.'

— 'I grew up in the suburb of a big town. We had moved to
Haarlem for that was 'so close to nature' . . . (My parents came
from Amsterdam!) Nature was always somewhere else. It
wasn't where we lived. One hour walking or two hours cycling
you always had to travel to get there. We were forced to go to
nature then . . . And I had to enjoy that for it was good or
healthy or something like that.' The workshop participant
describes this with a laugh and the group reacts to it in recognition. He continues: 'I found it terrible, we had to play in the
Bloemendaal "woods". It wasn't woods, it was more like a
park. That was "nice for Sunday afternoon" and I had to find it
nice. We lived beside the river. The water was dangerous, you
could fall into it but it wasn't nature! The bare little field across
from our house which was ideal for children to play in was not
nature. It was grass, a mess, pits, dandelions and: be careful!
We had a small garden in the back with sun in it. That wasn't
nature either. Flowers were put in it, we had to be careful with

those as well, this time not to damage them. I still have that. I live by the Amstel in Amsterdam. The trees that grow there I don't call nature, the river neither. It's water. Weird isn't it? As if I still have to go somewhere else, then it's nature . . .

'Now nature is for me primarily movement. Water especially but the earth too has movement.'

— 'For me nature is in everything, that's the way I grew up. I am part of it.'

And on a farm where children are taught about farm life I heard that there are city children who think milk comes from the shop . . . Understand me correctly: they think that milk is made there!

What the woman said about the respect for nature in countries like Peru has often been conveyed to us through literature and personal stories. As a matter of fact the second and the fourth answers come from women who are from other backgrounds than the original Dutch cultures and there too you notice a difference. That means that in their culture they are brought up with a far greater respect for the mutual connectedness of life than the average Dutch person is. We became further removed from nature because our way of life interfered. To discover the reciprocity and to be able to experience it. Receiving seems to be very, very difficult in our culture. Truly receiving from the heart without protesting and saying that you don't matter. And without feeling obliged to do something in return.

In the workshops we went on to look at how you direct your attention at things around you. From what point of view do you perceive? What is your starting point? An exercise to explore this can be done as follows:

Look at a plant or another natural object in front of you. Where is your attention? Are you thinking at all about what is in front of you or about something else?

Now focus your attention consciously *in* the plant and feel the effect of this on you.

Take time to feel this.

Next, direct your attention into the middle of your head and look at the plant from there. How is it different now from before?

Then aim your attention exactly between the plant and the middle of your head. Maybe you already get a sense of how you normally aim your attention at something. Where you perceive it from.

Practise this and feel the difference ever more clearly. Finally, let the attention of *the plant* there in front of you totally come at you and be aware of how that feels.

This fairly simple exercise can be useful for conducting more conscious communication with other life. By focusing your attention and directing it consciously you become more present in the here and now and you strengthen the energy of your attention, by which means the effect of the exchange grows a lot stronger. Your own emanation becomes much greater because of it and equally it empowers the radiance of the life form on which you focus your attention. In that moment there is nothing else but the plant and you. Well, actually you are hardly there either, for you are, as it were, focused in your attention!

The last part of the exercise is certainly important and we hardly ever consider that this too is possible. We tend to think that everything emanates from us humans. Why not turn this around? Everything that lives has a radiance and you can consciously tune in to it.

Then I ask people to go outside with all their senses open. Smell, feel, taste, watch, be 'sensual'. Nature too is completely sensual. She lacks a voice. She feels and radiates and vibrates.

Experiences:

— 'I felt a leaf with my hands and then with my lips. It was a totally different sensation. Unbelievable.'

This was followed by: 'When people are around I don't do it, and often I would just like to hug a tree. I do in fact do so, but first I check carefully that nobody is around.'

— 'When I'm in my little garden I do talk and give expression to my gratitude but just now I was receiving as well.'

Shame, yes of course. And you have to watch out that you don't get romantic and make up your own fairy-tales, that it remains real, for that is what we are talking about. For many people this temptation is great. I feel I have to warn you of that. The thing is, the real answers and experiences you get are always interesting and more unexpected than those you can think up yourself.

Perhaps the most important exercise is the one to open your heart. Through the usual misfortunes of life we have closed our hearts completely or partially to ourselves and to each other in order not to be hurt any more. Daring to let yourself be seen openly and honestly, simply as you are, with all your good and less nice sides, is hardly possible any more. We judge and sentence each other immediately and we do the same to ourselves. It is our defence, our weapon. How then, for heaven's sake, can one be open? In this process of feeling disappointed, undervalued, abandoned, our feelings too are shut off to a large degree. Your emotions are linked to your belly, your second chakra, which is often shut, closed. So to open it again to a tree or a flower is really difficult.

Those who have pets might be able to understand how it works because they know what safe and open contact is. Over the years of living with an animal trust develops and from it an alliance. You get to know its self-will. He or she becomes part of your home life. You took the animal *inside your house*. Into your life, inside your walls. A tree doesn't let himself be taken inside the house so easily! You do have plants in the house but you don't readily talk to them, let alone with them. You are 'allowed' to cuddle your dog, to have your cat on your lap and to talk to it, but talking to a plant is considered weird and when you hug a tree you are seen as completely nuts. And yet the tree or the plant is just as much present. He may indeed be outside your house but is just as alive and sensitive and as self-willed as the dog or the cat. Moreover, tree and plant as well as your pet animal will never be able to hurt you, simply because all they know is love. An animal can be scared, though, and lash out from fear. A tree, a flower, does not get scared and consequently they do not react from fear. They all react from feeling and with feeling.

The trees and flowers and stones and plants, water, the earth, the wind and the sun are the safest friends you can imagine. OK, the sun can burn you, the wind can turn into a hurricane, the earth can tremble, a tree can fall on top of you, water can sweep you away, but that never happens maliciously because that just simply is not possible. As you know, these nature elements have no free will! For them there is no 'right' or 'wrong' as in the human world, but then the question remains whether there really even is a 'wrong'. For them there is no yesterday or tomorrow. They live in the now. This too allows them to be non-judgemental.

Learning to open your heart once again to yourself and your non-judgemental surroundings is a wonderful exercise; it is curing, healing. In dialogue with our natural environment this opportunity to become whole is offered to us and we always overlook it. The loving attention we return is healing to *them* and *they* in their turn need this. It is not only we humans who need positive attention, but everything that lives.

Here is an exercise you can do to open your heart:
Go and sit in front of someone with whom you feel safe. At arm's length from each other. You agree who is number one and who is number two.

You both close your eyes and take time to feel yourself breathing calmly, you make contact with the earth through the soles of your feet and you feel your body sitting in the chair. In your mind make a circle around yourself. You are now sitting each in your own circle, in your chair, connected with the earth.

When you are centred in the knowledge that you are you and the other person there across from you is somebody totally different, then number one opens the circle in front of him- or herself and directs a beam of pure love, without thoughts, from the heart chakra, the chest, to the heart chakra of number two. Two opens his/her circle and heart chakra as well, further and further, and does *nothing but* receive the love. You need to have the feeling that it takes a ridiculously long time. Breathe deeply and *receive*. During all that time one of you keeps on radiating beams of love.

When you feel you have received down to the depths of your chest, and it can indeed take more than five minutes, only then do you return the love from that point to number one. Exactly in the same way: from your heart chakra to the chest, the heart chakra, of the other. Now all number one does is receive and nothing else but that. For a long time!

During this exercise there is *no talking,* only feeling. At the end, close your circle, both of you, so that you are once more in your own space and again direct your heart a bit more to yourself. Only after this do you discuss your experiences. Try to realise within yourself how it worked. Sometimes it just can't happen immediately. Too much panic, fear, sorrow, pain lies on top of it. Give yourself time to heal slowly through practice.

Now go outside, each of you alone. Feel which tree or flower is drawing your attention. As if it is inviting you to approach it. As if it is calling you in some way to do this exercise with you. At first it is quite a strange idea that a tree can invite you to come and stand with him/her. Yet it is so, just open yourself to it. Go and stand in front of it at arm's length and open your heart chakra to the pure love this tree is sending you. All you have to do is RECEIVE. Take as much time as you need for it and especially let your feelings be with it. Give your tears or any other emotion free rein when they come up. A tree can handle your fury and it transforms your energy.

When you feel that in your heart chakra you are full of the love for that other being, the flower or the tree, then from that point return the love. Feel as much as you are able to feel.

Naturally you may repeat this exercise with yet another element of nature that is drawing your attention and thus has something to share with you. You can practise this endlessly. Each time it will work a little more easily/naturally. Listen or watch.

Then, maybe right away, maybe later, when you are able to experience more and more, you may enter into communication with, for instance, the tree. Provided of course you feel like it. Ask and answer. Don't invent an answer; listen by opening up the way you did with your heart chakra and don't expect an answer: let yourself be surprised! It is truly always different from what you think it will be. Not least because the message is given from a space of unconditional love. Without judgement. Next, capture that answer or message in your heart as best you can. The more you exercise, the more you will hear, receive. And the more you are able to receive, the more you will be able to give.

How can you know that you are *not* interpreting or following your own thoughts?

From experience I know that, before you engage in any form of communication, it is important to start with yourself. Make contact with yourself, by feeling your body from the inside through your breathing, standing or sitting. Your feet on the earth and in contact with the earth on which they are standing. Next feel your own heart and open it inwards, to yourself, be it only a small crack. Only from there are you able to start the dialogue. Appreciation of yourself is part of the exchange and nature helps you to rediscover it. You can't leave yourself out when you are connecting with life that knows nothing except communicating from its own centre. The tree will never say: 'Oh forget it, I'm not important.' The tree is. Starting with yourself helps guard against interpreting and fantasising.

What happens to people is very beautiful. Here are some examples of participants who received a first assignment to go outside and engage in a conversation with a flower or a tree or one of the elements:

— 'I found it difficult to surrender to the flower and not make something up. There's a lot standing between us.'

— 'I had a beautiful contact with a flower. Inside it there was a fat hairy bumble-bee. I was standing there thoroughly enjoying it. It was as if the flower came closer and said: "Here, just enjoy me." In that way, you can simply hear it. Very moving and fantastic. I was given associations about myself and my daughter, very beautiful and healing. There we stood, the two of us, right in the middle of a field, beautiful and very vulnerable.'

— 'It takes quite a while to find the rhythm, the frequency, of the little flower. It is such a high energy that, for me, it is hardly perceptible. "You always overlook this, you might open your perception to this frequency," I then heard. Thereupon I received the assignment to walk around the whole garden and listen everywhere for this frequency. I associate this delicacy with something very small and vulnerable. But that didn't prove to be true at all. This energy was present in very different forms. Very unique.'

— 'It got too much. I had to shut myself off and felt a need to walk quite a distance to recover.'

— 'I went to look at moss. As a child I often looked for spots where there was moss, I found it so beautiful. Soft. I now asked how it is that I feel so attracted to moss. It said: "I transform the energy of the earth so that people can experience it and vice versa." I can imagine that this is a very attractive energy for a child.'

— 'It really does me good but, boy, is it hard work! I make a strong appeal to my heart and it hardly keeps up with it. The intense encounter with those small flowers touches so many levels. I thought it has a heavy energy, but I am heavy. The flower is light. I'm letting go of so much now. Good heavens, how good this is.'

— 'Only now do I understand the balance of yin and yang. All the flowers I see are contradictory. Each and every contradiction that can exist I see in the flowers. It's not easy to receive something, you have to do something for it. They are in balance, that strikes me. It doesn't matter how many small leaves or how they are hanging. It is infinite and it is nothing. In one single flower I saw sorrow. I found it disturbing. I didn't understand. I ran away from that, I'm not a therapist!'

— 'I was looking at the structure of the purple flower on that high stem and it reminded me strongly of flowers formed by coral. To the eye they have the same structure. I heard or felt that I had to give the image of the coral flower to this purple flower. That's what I did. Then I asked, "Is this what our contact is about now?" Yes, it was a part of it but there was more. I had to know that "by giving the image of the one flower to the other I, as a human being, was contributing to the consciousness of the unity of all life. This is not the same as contributing to the unity of consciousness. For that is not unified. It is contributing *to the consciousness of the unity*. An awareness that all living things are together when we think we are together."

'That I heard from the purple flowers. Verbena. I had never thought about it as such myself and now because of that I realise there is a lot more than one thinks. New channels are opening up in me. I also have a lot more in myself than I thought.'

— 'I went and stood in front of a chestnut tree and closed my eyes to shut it out. Then my feet started to tingle. The roots are giving it life, I thought. What is happening is logical.'

— 'I recovered a part that I was in danger of losing in the Netherlands. Namely that nature has a lot to offer you and can heal you as well. I was brought up to believe that and now I'm getting into contact with that part again. What I have done in this country is to focus more on people and now a balance is being restored within me. Both humans and nature can work in a healing way.'

— 'The chestnut tree by which I was standing has tumours of some kind. My first reaction: what a pity. Immediately I heard: "No, I don't want pity, I want respect. For respect is love and pity is not love. It is precisely our imperfections that make us unique."'

— 'During the meditation this morning I noticed that only with difficulty could I detach from death and what it means, for that is what is currently playing in my life. After the assignment it gradually changed. I went to a very fine small rosebud on a very thin green stem. It was growing out of an old part. Like a tree where leaves are falling, dying off, and where new fruits are growing. A message of balance there between dying off, leaving and renewal. That this is a circle, as it were. That it's all right.'

— 'I'm used to looking at something but now it is looking at me!'

— 'The river was calling me. I was sitting on a small bench and I saw the frequency of the water. On the surface it was quiet. Underneath it was different. Very vibrating, rich. It felt very healing, those layers of strength with which I had an intense connection. The ducks were being carried by the energy of the water, the boats too. The water was asking for respect, gratitude and attention. A lot of attention. The river wanted to have space, to become wider, vaster. As if it were afraid of drying up. It also clearly wanted to have contact with the cosmos, as if it had lost that.'

These are just a few examples; they are all so different that the temptation to write it all down is great. Nevertheless, I'm going to add one experience of my own:

This summer I was walking as usual in the mountains and a small purple pansy appeared in my path, in the middle of a wide valley, surrounded by a series of high rock-faces. It was clearly demanding my attention. I looked at it for a while. Then that little flower showed me her/his frequency, a very high bright frequency. And that very small, tiny pansy in the middle of these gigantic mountains said: 'Just watch, my energy is now with me but I can make it as vast as ever I want, as far as the mountains around me or further! I can do that on my own or we can do it together.' Apart from the message it gave me personally I was amazed that something so small and delicate can make itself so big whenever it wants to.

It is fascinating and baffling how, when you let yourself be drawn by an element from nature, that very element has something to teach you. The following day you will probably walk past it because this lesson, this wise teaching, is no longer necessary or because it's not the right time for it. It's really a loving interplay when you let it happen. But, understandably, precisely because of this it evokes resistance:

— 'I also want to be able simply to walk in the woods again. Just for a while I don't want to have anything to do with subtle energies any more, it's getting too much.'

— 'What I experience I cannot integrate in my body.'

— 'I think I have to be able to manage everything right away, whereas I want to take years processing all this.'

Regarding the more spiritual question about the relationships between the different levels of consciousness and the specific tasks of each life form on earth, so much information comes up during the meditation that we become totally enthusiastic.

The question was to look at the different specialities of stones, flowers, bushes and plants, animals and people. Here are some keywords to summarise what came up.

Stones:

Concentrated light forces;
healing;
on the one hand, keeping negative forces at bay; on the other hand, building stones;
solidity;
soil;
safety;
something to hold on to;
underground;
resting-point;
connection;
communication; at a vibration we don't hear, with other planets in the cosmos, each stone a unique vibration;
the vibration of the solidity of stones is of a kind which lies outside my perception;
they are a million years old and I am so young still in this one life;
so much is accumulated in a stone throughout time;
they are witnesses and guardians.

Flowers:

Bloom, colour, fragrance;
beauty;
taking care of joy and procreation;
giving colour;

enjoying;
healing;
zest for life;
communication with people on a heart level;
bringing 'de-light';
creation exists in order to enjoy;
tones too high to keep on following;
receiving;
welcome;
transformation of something heavy into something light;
singing choirs all over the world;
pinnacle of manifestation of essence for they go through the
process of birth, life and death in a short span of time.

Plants and bushes:

Protection;
strength;
relatedness;
cleansing;
connected with the earth's and our own pain;
communicating with what happens around us, love
and sorrow;
flow of life;
they screen things off;
connect horizontally;
give, also food;
cycle of coming and going;
contact between animal and human;
clothing of the earth;
earth power in relation to the air.

Trees:

Oxygen;
filtering;
refreshing;

breathing;
protection;
balance;
guardians;
teaching us humility in their greatness and to be great
in humility;
cosmos–earth connection;
wise;
supportive;
they give their fruits to the earth;
they teach us about being grounded, earthed;
rooted;
movement and immobility;
representatives of the qualities of the planets;
communication from firmness;
a base all over the world;
they are mutually connected with each other by species,
through the earth.

Animals:

Bringing people into contact with themselves;
food;
wisdom;
procreation;
maintaining a balance;
guardians;
cooperation;
example of the alternatives, the choices one can make;
they give the plant world a function;
they recognise the plant world;
carriers of widely diverging information;
mobility and perception;
group focus;
they give love;
group consciousness;
create equilibrium in imbalance;

playing with the earth;
connecting element between the different life forms.

Humans:

Renewers of process;
they cause chaos through which transformation
becomes possible;
helping the earth through changes;
giving and receiving love;
responsible for the whole;
making connections between light and dark, movement
and standstill;
seeing and being communication and thereby supporting
the process of transformation of the whole planet, keeping
it going and ourselves with it;
perception and awareness;
growth of individuality in order to achieve acceptance
of diversity;
freedom of choice, yes and no;
communication from movement out.

Beyond this the participants experience that certain trees
and plants go together, that there are connections. As natural
life groups. Interrelations in harmony and love, with respect
for changes within the overall constant change. Because the
harmony of the one influences the other. Harmony is not static and the earth is in constant change.

A few answers to the question: 'In which direction are we all
going?'

Regeneration;
as it goes in the cosmos so it goes in your body, the earth;
equilibrium, balance;
interrelations;

to further connect communication and interrelatedness;
to find new forms of balance;
we are a concert but with many discordant notes;
being more aware of each other, that choice you can make
every day anew, that is very rich;
being part of the whole.

People are discovering that there is more than they thought and that they themselves are so much more. They are beginning to see their surroundings in a different way and are experiencing that there is a lot to learn from life around us. Someone saw it as a giant figure eight which connected everything. For example, from mother and child to tree and cosmos, to animal and plant, to earth and sun. The order is unimportant, there are millions of connections in one whole. Wherein the earth, with all the life on it, is but a very small part of that whole. There is an open invitation to bring the connection to expression in your life, it is infinite.

The more spiritual or relating way I respond to the questions I have — once curious and now also anxious — is only one method to get in touch with everything that lives and remain so. This has brought me back to the wonder of life. The connection with everything opens up unthinkable possibilities.

But naturally there are many other paths to the unity and love around us. The different avenues of approach are useful and necessary. One person feels more attracted to the protection of animals and that is terribly important, for firstly each living being is entitled to live and who are we to take that away? And secondly it is a fact that when one species dies out it has drastic consequences for all life on earth. It disrupts a balance through which everything starts to slide.

Another person feels more attracted to the ecological movement which has made everybody aware that we have to deal more economically with our environment. Still others show enormous courage in militant action. They make and keep us aware so that we don't forget how harshly and ruthlessly we are destroying the silent life around us. So that we realise what, together, we are doing.

This book is intended as a humble yet conscious contribution to a greater awareness of the connection between everything that lives.

I sit back. It's five o'clock in the afternoon. I'm sitting outside in a gusting wind under a sky full of thunderclouds. I feel as small and vulnerable as the little pansy in the mountains. I could be crushed by a human foot just like that. And yet the little pansy knows no fear and radiates its power far over the mountains. I open myself up to the sun who appears from behind a gigantic dark-grey cloud and says: 'It's all right. You can release the book now.'

Bibliography

To finish, I am adding a categorised reading list to indicate some perspectives that are currently gaining attention. The books I mention can possibly be beacons in this immense, wide-ranging field for those who want to take their dialogue with nature further. Do know, though, that the real encounter can only take place from your feelings and through your own experiences. Not from your head or what happens for another! Yet reading about each other's experiences can be of great value and add something to our own perception.

Stories

Carter, Forrest, *The Education of Little Tree*, University of New Mexico Press, 1976
Redfield, James, *The Celestine Prophecy*, Bantam, 1994

Accounts of Experiences

Goelitz, Jeffrey, *Secrets from the Lives of Trees*, Planetary Publications, 1991
Greaves, Helen, *Testimony of Light*, Neville Spearman, 1989
Greaves, Helen, *The Challenging Light*, Neville Spearman, 1984
Miller, Lana, *Call of the Dolphins*, Rainbow Bridge Publishing, Portland, Oregon, 1989
Ocean, Joan, *Dolphin Connection: Interdimensional Ways of Living*, Dolphin Connection, 1989
Roads, Michael, *Talking with Nature*, HJ Kramer, 1988
Roads, Michael, *Journey into Nature*, HJ Kramer, 1990
Roads, Michael, *Journey into Oneness: a Spiritual Odyssey*, HJ Kramer
Small Wright, Machaelle, *Behaving As If the God in All Life Mattered: a New Age Ecology*, Perelandra, 1983

Experiences involving the Ancient Peoples

Andrews, Lynn, *Medicine Woman*, Penguin, 1989

Andrews, Lynn, *Flight of the Seventh Moon*, Penguin, 1989

Andrews, Lynn, *Jaguar Woman and the Wisdom of the Butterfly Tree*, HarperCollins, 1985

Andrews, Lynn, *Starwoman: We Are Made from the Stars and to the Stars We Must Return*, Warner Books, 1987

Castaneda, Carlos, *Power of Silence*, Simon & Schuster, 1987

Castaneda, Carlos, *Fire from Within*, Corgi, 1985

Morgan, Marlo, *Mutant Messages from Down Under*, Aquarian Press, 1995

Nau, Erika, *Huna Self-Awareness*, Samuel Weiser, 1992

Sams, Jamie & Carson, David, *Medicine Cards: The Discovery of Power Through the Ways of the Animals*, Bear & Co, 1988

Sams, Jamie, *Sacred Path Cards*, Bear & Co, 1951

Sun Bear/Wabun Wind/Crysalis Mulligan, *Dancing With the Wheel: the Medicine Wheel Workbook*, Simon & Schuster, 1991

Therapeutic

Raphaell, Katrina, *Crystal Enlightenment: the Transforming Properties of Crystals and Healing Stones*, Aurora Press, New York, 1985

Raphaell, Katrina, *Crystal Healing: the Therapeutic Application of Crystals and Stones*, Aurora Press, 1987

Anthroposophical

Steiner, Rudolf, *Nature Spirits*, R Steiner Publications, 1995

Scientific

Capra, Fritjof, *The Turning Point*, Bantam Books, 1982

Capra, Fritjof, *The Tao of Physics*, Fontana, 1992

Griffiths, Bede, *A New Vision of Reality*, HarperCollins, 1989

Jung, Carl Gustav, *Psychology and the East*, Ark Pubs., 1986

Kübler-Ross, Elisabeth, *On Death and Dying*, Macmillan, 1969

Kübler-Ross, Elisabeth, *Living With Death and Dying*, Souvenir Press, 1981

Naess, Arne, *Ecology, Community and Lifestyle*, Cambridge University Press

Sheldrake, Rupert, *Rebirth of Nature*, Rider, 1993

Sheldrake, Rupert, *The Presence of the Past*, Fontana, 1988

Stone, Robert B, *The Secret Life of Your Cells*, Schiffer, 1997

Tompkins, Peter & Bird, Christopher, *The Secret Life of Plants*, Penguin, 1975

Wilber, Ken, *No Boundary: Eastern and Western Apporaches to Personal Growth*, Shambhala, 1991

Zukav, Gary, *Seat of the Soul: Inspiring Vision of Humanity's Spiritual Destiny*, Century, 1991

Zukav, Gary, *Dancing Wu Li Masters*, Rider, 1991

Other titles from
Findhorn Press

NATURE SPIRITS & ELEMENTAL BEINGS
Marko Pogacnik

Although a lot has been written in recent years about nature spirits, this book by Slovenian author Marko Pogacnik is remarkable in that almost everything described in the book is based on his own practical experiences in communicating with these beings through meditation and tuning into plants, trees, animals and the landscape. He describes in detail the various elemental beings and their roles in maintaining the web of life, and also gives insights into related topics, such as the flow of energies within landscape, and the long-suppressed Goddess culture. His evocative images of the nature spirits draw our attention to the lost harmony of the natural world which has been disrupted by the impact of human culture.

£7.95 pbk 256 pages • ISBN 1 899171 66 5

THE GOLDEN WEB
Gwennie Armstrong Fraser

The Golden Web is a symbol of the divine consciousness embracing Nature and humanity, infusing everything with its radiance and power. The divine Light glows at the centre of the web and radiates outwards, sustaining and illuminating all life. Each being and life form has a place within the interconnected whole. This book describes the urgent need for a new partnership with Nature through the messages from the Devic level of consciousness. The devas explain the levels of consciousness which we share with Nature and the profound beauty and light with which all life is created. They urge us to step forward together, deepen our connection with the natural world, and take active steps to begin the process of ecological restoration. In this book we can each discover our role.

£6.50 pbk 160 pages • ISBN 1 899171 25 8

THE FINDHORN GARDEN
The Findhorn Community

Beautifully illustrated, this book tells the story of the early days of the Findhorn Community and its communications with the nature intelligences or 'devas' underlying the physical forms of plants, trees and landscapes.

£9.95 pbk 196 pages • ISBN 0 905249 70 4

Amazonian Gem & Orchid Essences
Andreas Korte, Antje & Helmut Hofmann

From the heart and lungs of our planet, the vibratory qualities of the local gems and orchids have been extracted for their therapeutic effects. This book describes each of the essences and its application

£9.95 pbk 116 pages (inc. 40 detachable colour cards) • ISBN 1 899171 91 6

Findhorn Flower Essences
Marion Leigh

These flower essences have been developed over several years, and now their uses in the healing of humanity and the planet are described in this beautiful book.

£7.95 pbk 146 pages (inc. 16 in full colour) • ISBN 1 899171 96 7

Australian Bush Flower Essences
Ian White

An informative yet personal picture of fifty bush flower essences and detailed information about their preparation and use in all areas of healing. Fully Illustrated. The Australian Bush Flower Essences themselves are available in the UK and many other countries.

£11.95 pbk 210 pages (inc. 16 in full colour) • ISBN 0 905249 84 4

My Life My Trees
Richard St Barbe Baker

Conservationist, forester, founder of 'Men of the Trees', Richard St Barbe Baker was by any account a remarkable man. He worked with President Roosevelt to establish the Civil Conservation Corps, involving six million youths. More recently he started the 'Save the Redwoods' campaign in California and was instrumental in the planting of over 26 trillion trees internationally by organisations he founded or helped. This book tells his life story.

£5.95 pbk 168 pages • ISBN 0 905249 63 1

For a complete catalogue of Findhorn Press books and products, please fill in this order form and send to:

Findhorn Press
The Park
Findhorn
Forress
Moray
Scotland IV36 0TZ
fax +44 (0)1309 690036
email thierry@findhorn.org

or

Findhorn Press Canada
102-2250 Fraser Street
Vancouver
Canada V5T 3T8
fax 604-879-3942
email whittam@unixg.ubc.ca

Name_____

Address _____

_____

_____

Post Code/Zip _____

My special interests are _____

_____

I particularly enjoyed reading *Dialogue with Nature* because

_____

_____

_____

_____